Plan

■ Notice Board

▲ Cross Section

● Perspective: Germany

024

RA
Holiday houses in Pedras Salgadas
Photo Ricardo Oliveira Alves

052

Atelier Tekuto
House in Kamagaya
Photo Toshihiro Sobajima

076

Herzog & de Meuron
Elbe Philharmonic Hall in Hamburg
Photo Axel Schmies

Long Section

092

Wiel Arets
Photo Erwin Olaf

156

TAO
Viewing Platform on Hill in Weihai
Photo Yao Li

126

Form
House in Otsu
Photo Takumi Ota

146

XTH
House in Berlin
Photo Anja Büchner

ATRIUM
Our modular process
makes your building a snap.
Geometrica®
architecture.geometrica.com

MARK

Subscribe and save up to 42% off the cover price
Visit frameweb.com/mark to get the best deal.

Back Issues
Buy online at frameweb.com/store

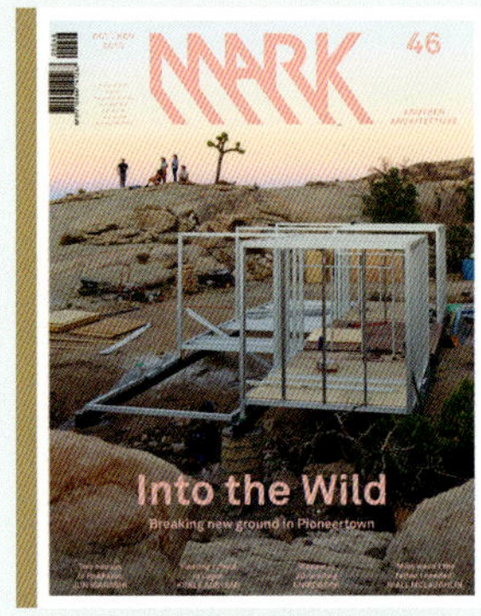

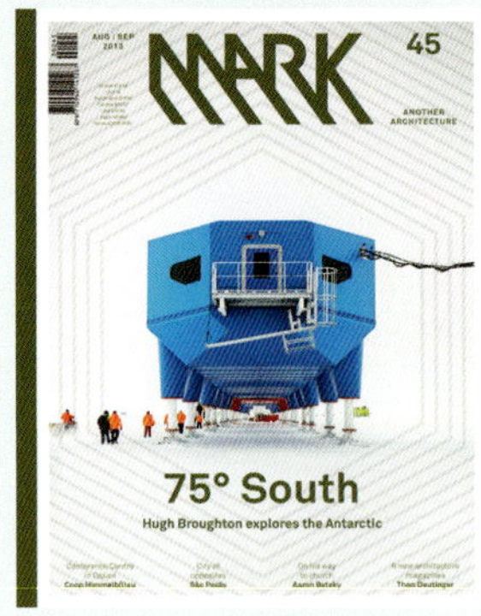

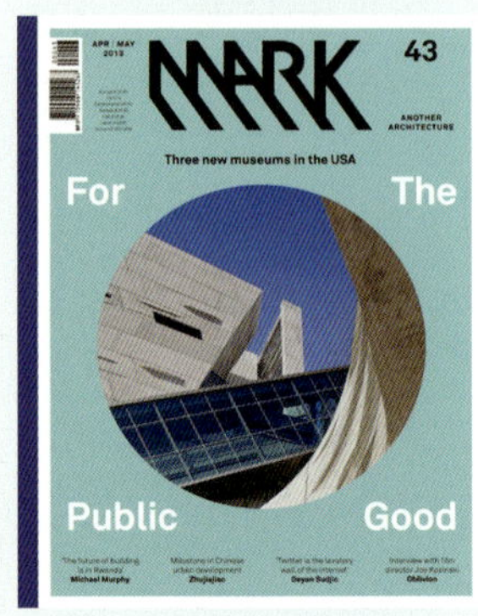

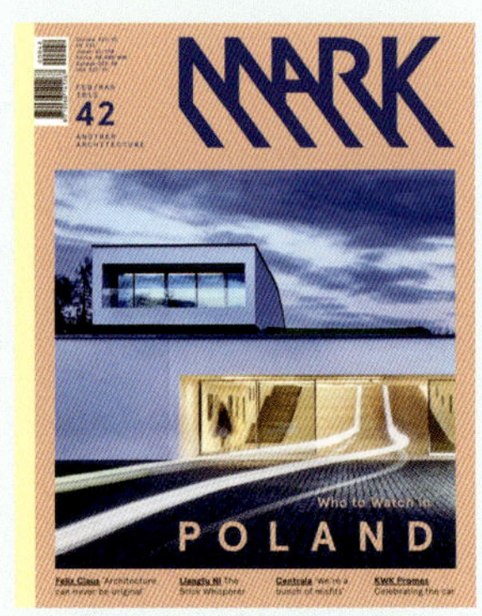

Mark is published 6 times a year by

Frame Publishers
Laan der Hesperiden 68
1076 DX Amsterdam
T +31 20 330 0630
F +31 20 428 0653
mark@frameweb.com
www.frameweb.com

Editorial
Editor in Chief
Arthur Wortmann
arthur@frameweb.com

Editor
David Keuning
david@frameweb.com

Editorial Intern
François-Luc Giraldeau
francois@frameweb.com

Contributing Editors
Thomas Daniell, Grant Gibson, Florian Heilmeyer, Cathelijne Nuijsink, Katya Tylevich, Michael Webb

Copy Editors
InOtherWords (D'Laine Camp, Donna de Vries-Hermansader)

Design Director
Barbara Iwanicka

Designers
Mariëlle van Genderen
Cathelijn Kruunenberg

Design Intern
Federica Ricci

Translators
InOtherWords (Donna de Vries-Hermansader, Christine Gardner, Pierre Bouvier), Kimberly Bradley

Contributors to this issue
Ursula Baus, Anneke Bokern, Theo Deutinger, Kirsten Hannema, Falk Jaeger, Ana Martins, Pulane Mpotokwane, Bert de Muynck, Alexandra Onderwater, Sergio Pirrone, Jane Szita, Masaaki Takahashi, Dan Wood, Oliver Zeller

Printing
Tuijtel

Lithography
Edward de Nijs

Cover photography
Marcus Bredt

Publishing
Directors
Robert Thiemann
robert@frameweb.com
Rudolf van Wezel
rudolf@frameweb.com

Circulation Director
Benjamin Verheijden
benjamin@frameweb.com

Sales Director
Elles Middeljans
elles@frameweb.com

Account Manager
Nienke van der Maar
nienke@frameweb.com

Online Advertising
Nikki Brandenburg
nikki@frameweb.com

Finance
Diana Gremmen
diana@frameweb.com
Cedric Isselt
cedric@frameweb.com

Advertising Representatives
Italy
Studio Mitos
Michele Tosato
michele@studiomitos.com
T +39 0422 894 868

Turkey
Titajans
Hilmi Zafer Erdem
titajans@titajans.com
T + 90 212 257 76 66

Subscriptions
service@frameweb.com

Subscription Rates
Including VAT and postage. To subscribe, visit www.frameweb.com/mark

1-year (6 issues): € 99
1-year student* (6 issues): € 79
2-year (12 issues): € 188

* valid only with a copy of your student registration form

Bookstore Distributors
Mark is available at sales points worldwide. Please see frameweb.com/magazines/where-to-buy

Mark (ISSN#1574-6453) is published bi-monthly by Frame Publishers and distributed in the USA by DSW, 75 Aberdeen Rd, Emigsville PA 17318. Periodicals postage paid at Emigsville PA. Send address changes to Mark, c/o PO Box 437, Emigsville PA 17318-0437.

Notice Board

↑ **Culture Container, New Busan Tower**
Busan | South Korea
Kim Byungchan (Dong-A Univ.) and Eunkyung Lee (EMA Architects)
Landmark in Yongdusan Park to replace the 40-year-old Busan Tower
Proposal

← **Show Under Skin**
Riga | Latvia
NRJA and IG Kurbads
Riga Theatre reconstruction
Competition entry, honourable mention
nrja.lv
Rendering by Linda Leitāne-Šmīdberga

↓ **Petersen Automotive Museum**
Los Angeles | CA | USA
Kohn Pedersen Fox Associates (KPF)
Refurbishment of the museum's current building on Wilshire Boulevard
Expected completion early 2015
kpf.com

← **Changing the Face**
Warsaw | Poland
Pruthiphon Buakaew (Titiwat Uboltham, Kasama Yingyodyeam and Pruthiphon Buakaew)
Memorial to the 49 victims of a 1979 explosion that badly damaged Bank Polski's Rotunda office. The proposal preserves 45 existing columns and adds four for a total of 49
Competition entry
pruthiphon.com

↙ **Live Between Buildings**
Copenhagen | Denmark
Mateusz Mastalski and Ole Robin Storjohann
Infill between two existing buildings, designed for New Vision of The Loft 2, an international design competition organized by roof-window manufacturer Fakro
Competition entry, first prize

↓ **Cristal Riviera**
Rennes | France
Périphériques Architectes, A/LTA and Hamonic + Masson
Offices, cinema and restaurants in the Ilot Féval area of EuroRennes
Competition entry
peripheriques-architectes.com
a-lta.fr
hamonic-masson.com
Rendering by Luxigon

→ **GWA Tower**
Beijing | China
DOS Architects
Cantilevering courtyard tower in the Lize Financial Business District housing a hotel, office space, retail and residential units
Competition entry, first prize, expected completion 2017
dosarchitects.com

↘ **Project Jewel**
Singapore
Benoy
Mixed-use lifestyle complex to be built at Singapore Changi Airport
Expected completion undisclosed
benoy.com

↓ **Oast**
Kent | UK
Acme (Nicholas Channon, Deena Fakhro, Friedrich Ludewig, Heidrun Schuhmann)
Residential design based on oast houses, or hop kilns, which are used in the process of brewing beer
Proposal
acme.ac

↑ **National Gallery of Indonesia**
Jakarta | Indonesia
Erick Kristanto, Kenneth Sit and Daniel Hui
Redevelopment of the National Gallery of Indonesia, including preservation of two heritage buildings
Competition entry

→ **Composite Building**
Hong Kong | China
Aedas
Serviced apartment building at No. 78-88 Sai Yee Street
Expected completion 2016
aedas.com

↓ **Dawang Mountain Resort**
Changsha | China
Coop Himmelb(l)au
The Deep Pit Ice and Snow World features a winter sports resort with an indoor ski slope, a water park, a restaurant and shops
Competition entry, first prize, expected completion undisclosed
coop-himmelblau.at

↑ **Sächsische AufbauBank**
Leipzig | Germany
Acme (Felicity Brouwers, Delphine Körner, Katharina Kohlroser, Friedrich Ludewig, Isabel de la Mora, Heidrun Schuhmann)
Development bank of Saxony, accommodating a staff of 600 and including a conference centre, a cafeteria, parking facilities and a new public space
Competition entry, first prize
acme.ac

↖ **Red Hill Rise**
Prague | Czech Republic
Maxwan and MS Architekti
A mixed-use complex above an underground station, Red Hill Rise consists of offices and retail
Expected completion undisclosed
maxwan.com
msgroup.cz

← **Tour Amazonie**
Nantes | France
A/LTA (Jean-Luc Le Trionnaire, Alain Tassot, Maxime Le Trionnaire, Gwénaël Le Chapelain)
152 apartments (72 private and 79 social), an activity area and parking facilities
Expected completion 2015
a-lta.fr
Rendering by FOZR

15:45
Office building, Paris
Smart, flexible solutions for the buildings of today – and tomorrow
Quick, comfortable movement combined with reliable security and access control. Meeting these conflicting demands is no easy task. Our answer? KONE People Flow Intelligence – smart, flexible solutions for access and destination control, information communication, and equipment monitoring.
kone.com/peopleflowintelligence
Access
Information
KONE People Flow Intelligence
Destination
Monitoring
Dedicated to People Flow™
KONE
B

← **Life Aquatech**
London | UK
ThinkTank (Armando Bussey, Edward Luckman, Vichayuth Meenaphant, Ana Margarita Wang-Zuniga)
Building with a fibreglass shell that collects and distributes water in a soft expandable silicone membrane
Proposal
thinktankaadrl.com

← **Shanshui City**
Beijing | China
Ma Yansong
Incorporating natural forms, Shanshui City is a lakeside office and residential complex in Chaoyang Park
Proposal
i-mad.com

↙ **161-165 Clarence Street**
Sydney | Australia
Koichi Takada Architects
Mixed-use, 24-storey tower with retail space and serviced apartments
Proposal
koichitakada.com
Rendering by Simon Perry | Integrated Design Solutions

↓ **Office Tower**
New York | NY | USA
MA2 (Michael Arellanes II)
Office tower in Manhattan's South Street Seaport, with an adjacent parking garage
Proposal
m-a-2.com

Symbol of strength Even the smallest change has great potential – USM adds the expression to each transformation.

Request detailed information or visit our showroom.

International: USM U. Schärer Söhne AG, 3110 Münsingen Switzerland, Phone +41 31 720 72 72
USA: USM U. Schaerer Sons Inc., 28–30 Greene St., New York, NY 10013, Phone +1 212 371 1230
Showrooms: Berlin, Bern, Düsseldorf, Hamburg, Munich, New York, Paris, Stuttgart, Tokyo
info@usm.com, www.usm.com

USM
Modular Furniture

neue räume 13

International
Interior Design Exhibition
Zurich-Oerlikon
27th Nov. to 1st Dec. 2013
ABB event hall 550

www.neueraeume.ch

Wed	Thu	Fri	Sat	Sun
27th Nov.	28th Nov.	29th Nov.	30th Nov.	1st Dec.
12 pm – 9 pm	12 pm – 9 pm	12 pm – 9 pm	10 am – 9 pm	10 am – 8 pm

Media Partner

annabelle

ARCHI TONIC

swiss-architects.com

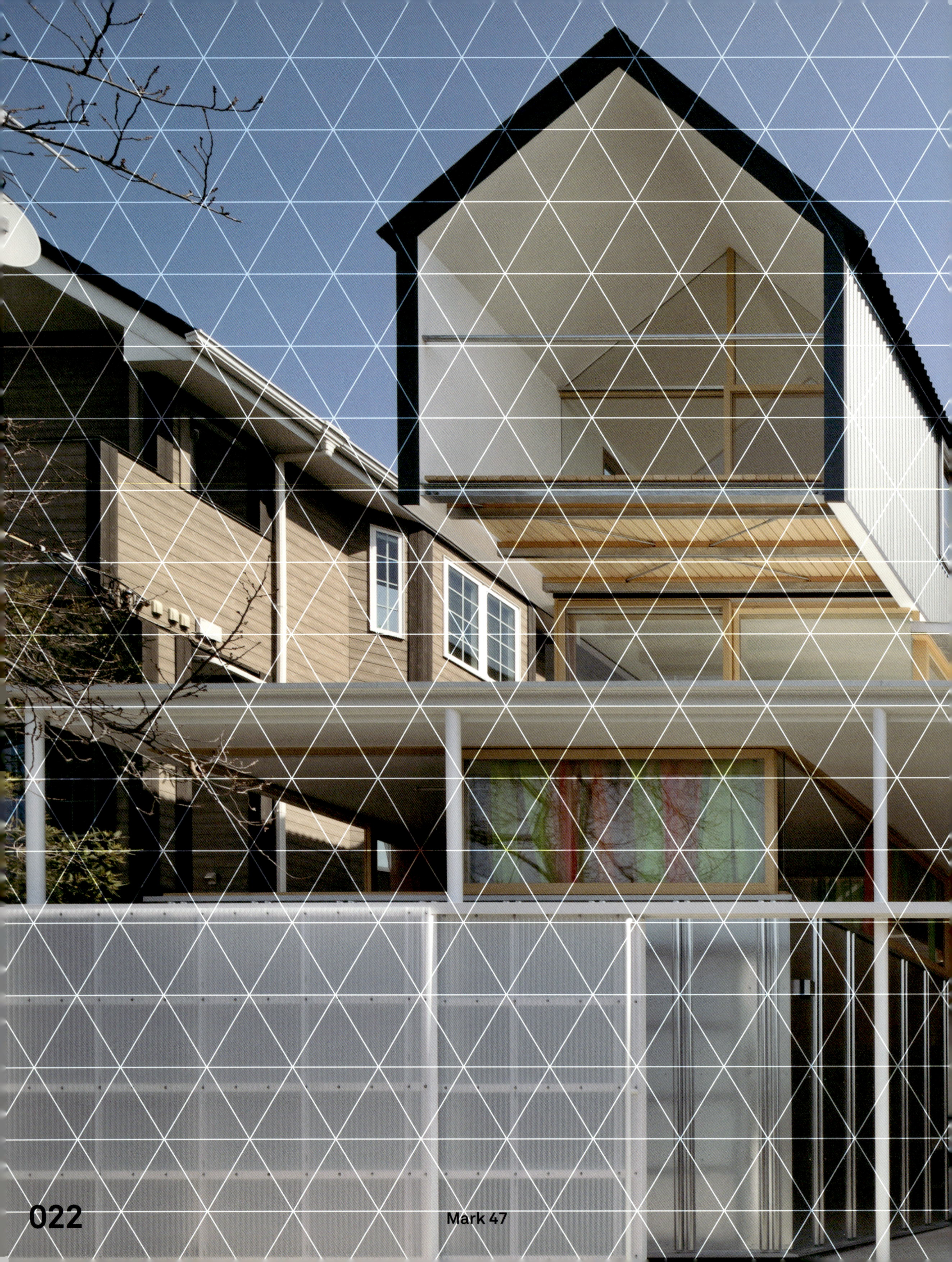

Cross Section

RA **reimagines the tree house**

Text **Pulane Mpotokwane**
Photos **Ricardo Oliveira Alves**

A long path draws you over a footbridge to the entrance of a small house. On an elevated structure, among the leaves of the trees, you feel even higher than you are, as your eye follows the descent of the slope below. Inside, skylights and windows dominate an all-white studio. Everything is pristine. The atmosphere is meditative and ethereal, almost spiritual. The bed is the centrepiece of the room – a podium from which to gaze up at the treetops, sky and stars.

This is the experience architects Luís and Tiago Rebelo de Andrade of RA crafted for guests at their Tree Snake Houses in Pedras Salgadas Park. Collaborating with their clients, they began a mission to reignite eco-tourism in Portugal, which had its heyday in the early 1900s before holidaymakers forsook forests for the beach.

In an effort to lure people back to the woodlands, RA drew inspiration from the archetypal forest dwelling: the tree house. 'The tree house is something each of us wished to have when we were little,' says Luís, 'a place that lives in our imaginations.' Wanting to re-create that childhood fantasy, the team at RA designed a contemporary treetop retreat. There was just one problem: they did not have permission to fasten anything to the trees in the park. Instead, they designed two freestanding structures and attached the houses to them in one day.

The trees do have a nonphysical connection to the buildings, though. As Tiago explains, cladding materials used for the Tree Snake Houses include the same dark wood that grows in the park, to ensure the buildings remain 'in symphony with the trees'. Locally sourced, the timber integrates fully into its environment, becoming almost invisible, and will, as Luís affectionately puts it, 'grow old with dignity'.

The white interior acts as a neutral backdrop to the greens and browns of the trees, allowing views of the outdoors to be the focus of the houses. The light colour also helps the tiny 25-m² studios to feel bigger than they are.

All of RA's projects are designed to show respect for their contexts. 'We are in an era in which architects are producing sculpture,' says Luís. 'In this globalized age we should try to reinforce the identity of place. Otherwise, it's going to be a boring world where everything is the same. I think we can achieve identity if we feel the place, respect the place and work with the materials of the place.'

rebelodeandrade.com

The bed is a podium from which to gaze up at the treetops.

Plan

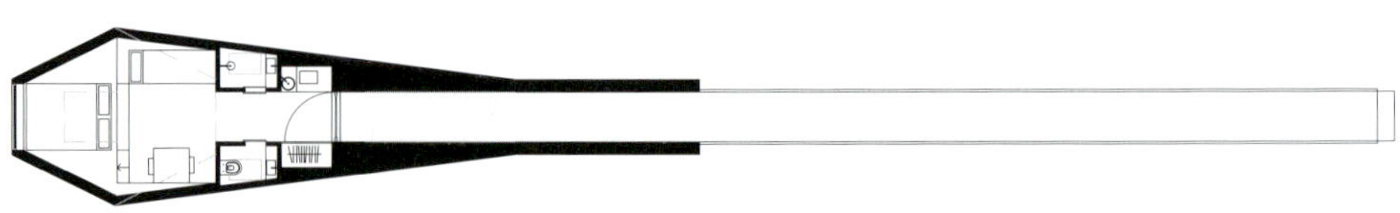

Studio Dasar **carefully extends a cultural centre**

Text **Bert de Muynck**
Photos **Davy Linggar**

Completed in less than two years, Anjung Salihara is the first project by young Indonesian architect Danny Wicaksono of Studio Dasar. The building is the latest addition to the existing Komunitas Salihara, a cultural centre consisting of a black-box theatre and an art gallery. Wicaksono's contribution rises from a small site between the cultural complex and its informal surroundings. It accommodates dance-rehearsal and recording studios, audiovisual facilities, guest rooms for resident artists and other visitors, an archive space and an open-air amphitheatre. In order to fit a 1450-m^2 programme into a plot of land measuring only 200 m^2, the architect was forced to design a multistoreyed building.

'I wanted the building to integrate with the existing buildings of the arts centre, both in appearance and access,' Wicaksono says, 'so it seemed only reasonable to opt for a grey exterior, but I chose a different finish, which gives Anjung Salihara a slightly different texture.' It was important to consider the neighbourhood when designing the back of the structure. 'Here, the building faces a residential area, and I wanted to provide people with a nice view – definitely nothing too acrobatic. I think of this extension as the "second façade" of the cultural complex.' The building has a rounded form and is punctuated with wood-framed windows that are equipped with louvres, allowing for an optimal circulation of air and thus a reduction in energy consumption.

studiodasar.com

+ 1

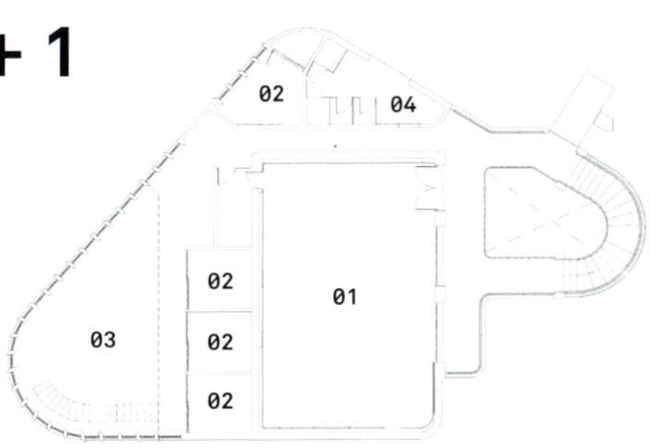

+ 2

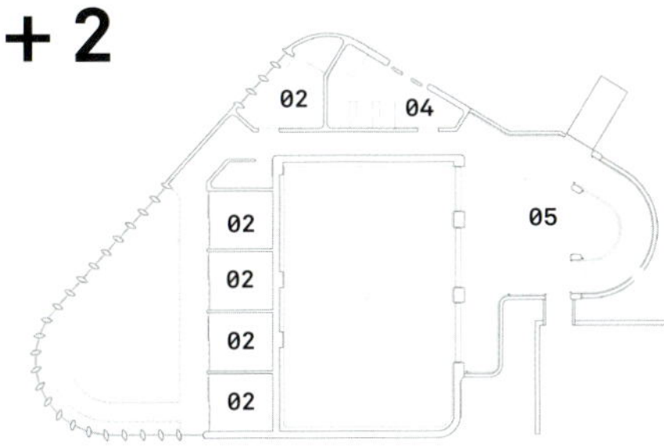

+ 3

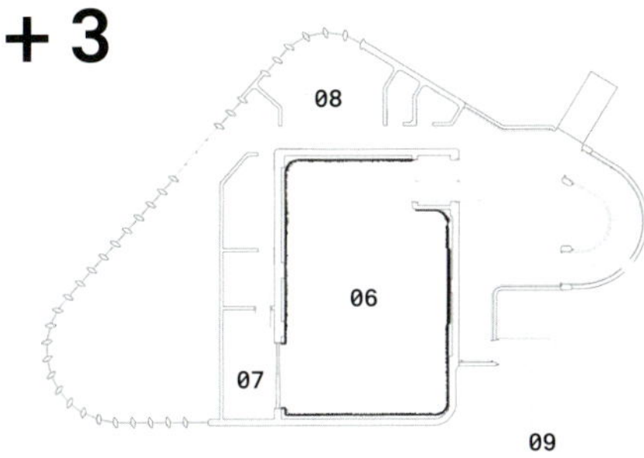

01 Dance studio
02 Guest room
03 Lounge
04 Bathroom
05 Terrace
06 Music studio
07 Recording studio
08 Gym
09 Bridge to theatre

Aleksi Briclot and Michel Koch terraform Paris

Text **Oliver Zeller**
Images **Dontnod Entertainment**

Remember Me, an action puzzler from developer Dontnod Entertainment and Capcom, immerses gamers in Paris, 2084. Orwellian corporation Memorize has gained control over a populace that uses its Sensen implants to upload, share and remove memories.

The player traverses this futuristic Paris as Nilin, an elite memory hunter. Nilin is able to enter a person's mind surreptitiously, locate a past event adrift in a spatial sea of memories, and rewrite her victim's recollection of that moment. Following her escape from Bastille Prison, Nilin and her fellow Errorists pursue a plan to take down Memorize.

Paris, now Neo-Paris, has undergone yet another reformation akin to its modernization by Baron Georges-Eugène Haussmann in the second half of the 19th century. In 2084, Haussmann's rational design – featuring stretches of wide boulevards with carefully regulated building façades – has regressed in some areas into a maze of industrialized alleys comparable to those of medieval Paris.

What's most striking about Neo-Paris is its verticality. Early on, visitors find themselves peering up at neoclassical buildings: even the Basilica of the Sacré Cœur appears to be a skyscraper among a forest of skyscrapers. Art Director Aleksi Briclot explains this peculiarity in *The Art of Remember Me* (2013): 'Previous wars have left enormous scars in the Neo-Paris landscape. Bombs that penetrated into the groundwater caused local landslides in different areas', ruining the Métro and 'resulting in the destroyed pockets that became Deep-Paris'. The architecture here is an eclectic mix, where even a ship run aground in the wake of rising seas was 'in typical Deep-Paris fashion, recycled into a habitable space'.

Mid-Paris features Haussmann-era architecture with high-tech extensions reminiscent of Foster + Partners' work on the Hearst Tower in New York City. 'Typical streets with cafés, brasseries, apartments and patios connect the setting to the Paris of today', even as augmented-reality signs sprout from shops and offices where humanoid robots work, while drones hover overhead.

The skyscrapers of High-Paris mark a return to Haussmann's philosophies with wider, more geometrically organized spaces that incorporate 'strong lines and diagonals in order to visually express the concept of order', despite the chaos below.

Early in the game, Nilin steals codes from the city's leading architect to open the Saint-Michel Dam, one of many hidden dams that stem the rising waters caused by global warming. Flooding the district, the player has in a sense further terraformed the city. Neo-Paris invites planners and architects to speculate on ways to deal with the drastic changes poised to besiege future urban environments.

Jeffrey Inaba **strikes up the band**

Text **Dan Wood**
Photos **Greg Irikura**

The idea of a pop-up music academy is strange enough. That it was sponsored by Red Bull and designed by uber-intellectual Jeffrey Inaba crosses into the possibly bizarre. The result, however, is a pure poetry of sight and sound, geometry and colour, punctuated by a sincere undertone of the unexpected. In fact, what makes the space so surprisingly good is its complete lack of either over-theorized pretension or stifling corporate messaging. It seems to be, truly, all about the music.

The 3,500-m^2 Red Bull Music Academy New York is spread over four floors of an old Chelsea warehouse. The upper floors feature a squiggly plan that creates collaborative music pods and an open office that contains an enormous x-shaped worktable. The public programme on the ground floor and in the basement – including recording studios and a radio station – is where Inaba's finely honed sense of geometry and colour are cranked up to eleven. His best trick is combinations of ellipses in plan and section. Where they meet orthogonal walls, corners and edges make alcoves and rooms that blend into curving surfaces and walls humming with precision.

Ancillary spaces throb with saturated reds, oranges, purples and yellows. Downstairs, as you move from a bright white lobby to a cloud-shaped room – in black, with a constellated ceiling – you're literally dragged forward in anticipation of what may lie beyond the next corner.

Inaba had a great backing band. Graphic designer Glen Cummings (MTWTF) and lighting designer Suzan Tillotson contributed clever graphic treatments and custom neon-fluorescent light fixtures. Technical assistance was provided by Slab Architecture and engineering by Buro Happold and Kam Chiu. With Inaba leading, the team discovered a unique groove and recorded a vibrant piece of interior architecture for the city.

inaba.us

+7

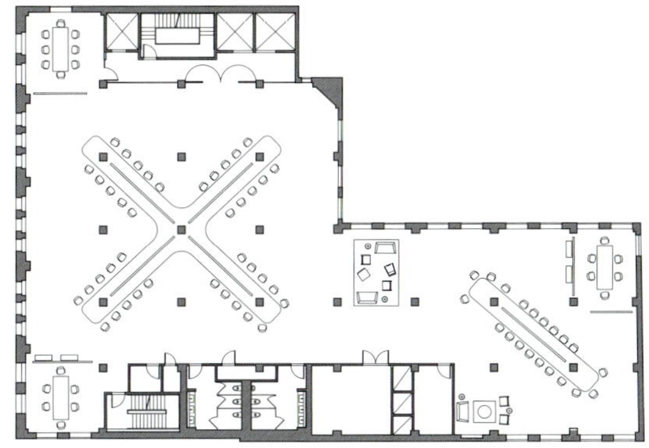

+6

0

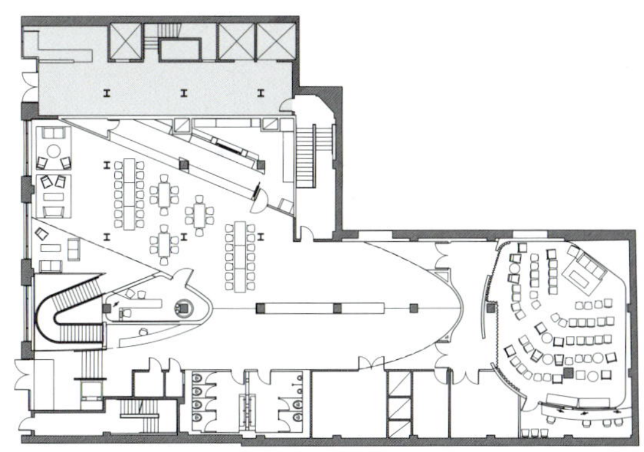

-1

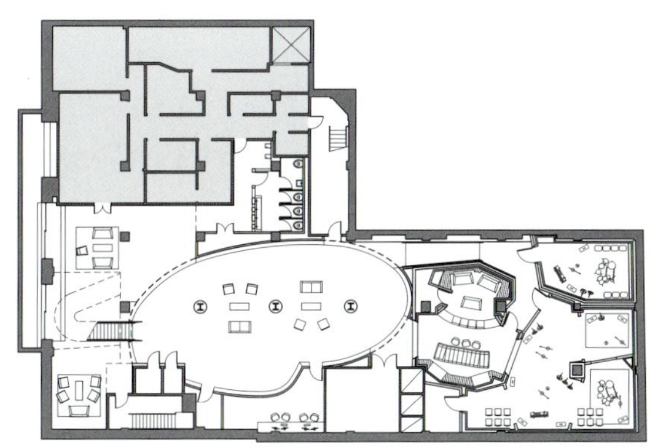

McDowell +Benedetti **swings through Hull**

Text **Pulane Mpotokwane**
Photo **Timothy Soar**

McDowell+Benedetti's Scale Lane Bridge over the River Hull is fast becoming a destination in its own right. Jonathan McDowell tells us more about the project.

Was urban regeneration part of the brief or an ingredient added by your team?

JONATHAN MCDOWELL: Urban regeneration was the purpose of the brief. The bridge is part of a master plan to regenerate the city and link the river – which is little used – to the main parts of Hull.

How did you arrive at the form of the bridge?

The form comes from the constraints of the Hull. It's an unusual river – half of it is mud and half is water. The brief required an opening bridge, and in this context the most economical design was a swing bridge. We fixed the counterbalance of the bridge in the muddy part and cantilevered the opening half. The spiral shape comes from the fact that the length of the ramp that we needed was longer than the span of the river, so we had to curve the route.

So the shape wasn't based on the silhouette of a ship?

That's the illusion at the back of one's mind, but we didn't design it that way. It does have that quality, though.

This design is part amusement ride, part bridge. What do you think is the most important aspect of the project if you had to pick one?

Well, it is a bridge. But if I have to pick, I'd call the project a 'place' – a new place worth a visit in its own right, which is not always the case for bridges.

Is there something you think people should know about the bridge that is not obvious from photographs or drawings?

One thing you can't get from photos is the experience of being on the bridge when it opens. It's a calm, serene, majestic ride – not clanky or noisy, as you might expect. It was a hugely complex piece of engineering to design and construct. It's so heavy, but beautifully smooth.

mcdowellbenedetti.com

Project: Oregon Employment Department
Location: Salem, Oregon
Architect: Hennenbery Eddy Architects
Photographer: Sally Painter

Woven Wire Drapery

Cascade Coil Drapery's flexible round weave woven wire fabrics are catching the eyes of today's architects and interior designers. With its versatility, unique texture and variety of colors, Cascade Coil Drapery is a long term solution for today's residential and commercial projects. Besides being durable, fireproof, and virtually maintenance-free, the material diffuses and enhances lighting without blocking views or ventilation. Save energy by reducing heat loss and gain using Cascade Coil's woven wire fabric for interior and exterior window applications. For over 25 years, Cascade Coil has offered round weave woven wire fabrics that have fueled the imagination of architects, interior designers and other creative minds in the design community.

Cascade Coil proudly manufactures their products in the USA and distributes them globally.

CASCADE COIL DRAPERY®

www.cascadecoil.com | T+1.971.224.2188

Text **Cathelijne Nuijsink**
Photos **Shinkenchiku-Sha**

Why this jumble of building materials and textures in one house?

YO SHIMADA (Tato Architects): When designing, I always look for a positive way to interpret the surrounding environment. This house is in a residential area that was developed in the 1930s, and it sits on a slope. From the site, we can see a kind of mosaic of old and renovated houses from different periods and generations, each with a personal history. To coordinate my design with this hotchpotch of housing styles – from 1930 right up to the present – I used a step-by-step design method of accumulation. That is to say, the rough-textured concrete walls and retaining wall of my design match masonry walls and

Tato **reveals the richness**

The structure is an accumulation of different housing styles.

Long Section

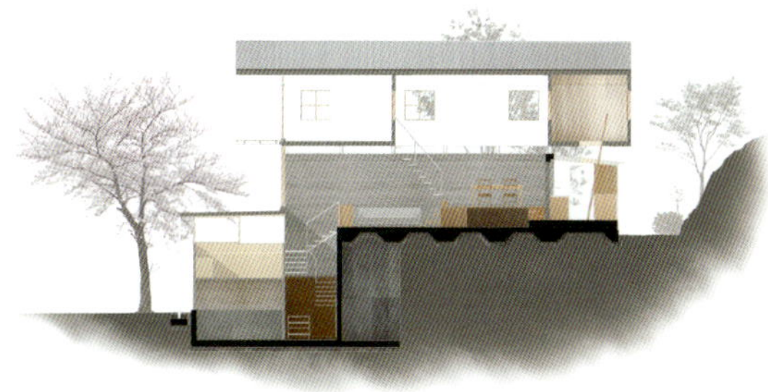

concrete walls belonging to the oldest buildings in the neighbourhood. My project is topped by an archetypal house with a pitched roof similar to that of surrounding roofs. At a lower level, I opted for a thin flat roof in white, which represents contemporary architecture. The boxy structure at ground level is clad in the same kind of steel panelling that is often used for temporary safety enclosures at building sites, giving the impression that the house itself is still under construction.

To design this house, I set out to rethink the entire residential area. This strategy suggests that it might be wise for architects to take a much closer look at the richness hidden in the diversity of historical eras that make up a neighbourhood.

tat-o.com

of the neighbourhood

+2

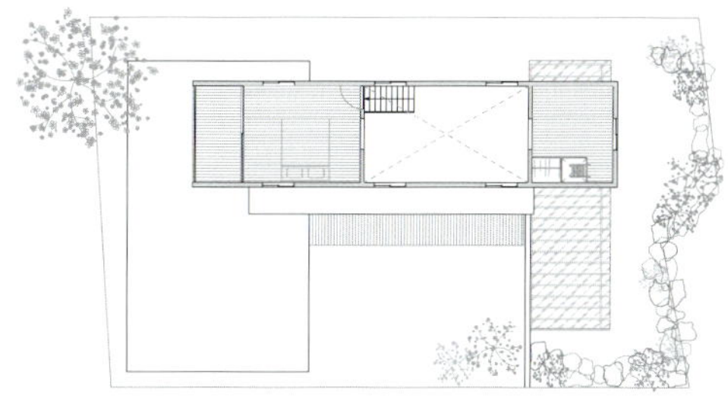

+1

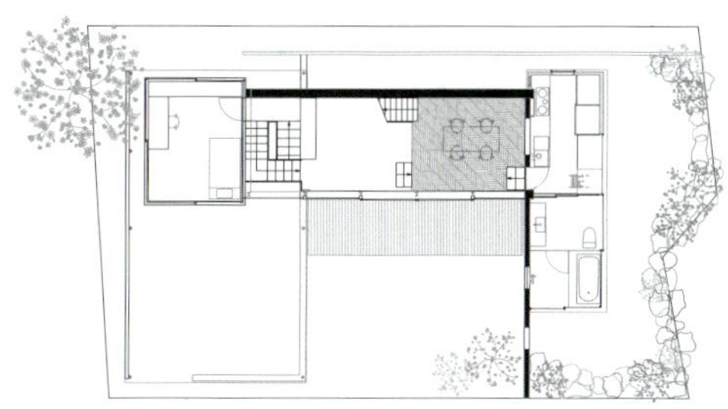

0

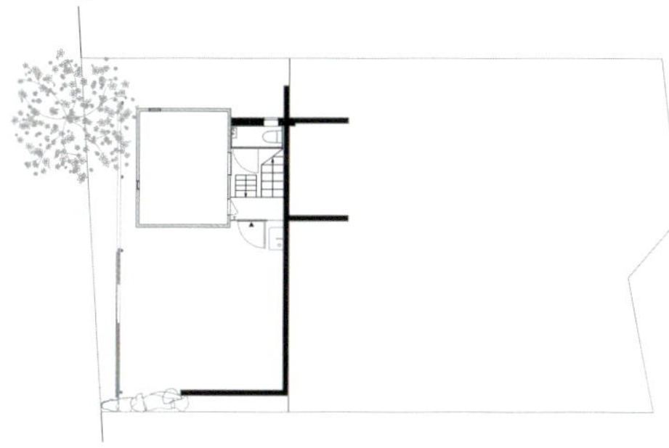

Phil Ivey **and** Syd Mead **take the McMansion into space**

Text **Oliver Zeller**
Images **Sony Pictures**

Director Neill Blomkamp follows up on 2009's Academy Award-nominated alien-apartheid film *District 9* with the similarly allegorical *Elysium*. In *Elysium*, sociopolitical commentary shifts to issues of wealth discrepancy and immigration. Earth, stripped of its resources, is now a place of squalor, a giant favela. The film follows Matt Damon as Max, an orphan and former gang member turned factory worker who is ultimately forced to find a way onto Elysium, a space station where the ultra affluent live in luxury and perfect health.

The director, working initially with a small team of concept artists from Weta Workshop and later with production designer Phil Ivey and visual futurist Syd Mead, has created a satirical view of what Earth could become – a view that offers a veiled commentary on the socioeconomic forces that influence and co-opt architecture.

A highly striking image early in the film depicts the slums of Los Angeles, with skyscrapers taken over by squatters. Makeshift platforms, conduits and huts grow haphazardly off tall, half-gutted buildings like parasites. It's as if the now-defunct Kowloon Walled City had taken over all of Hong Kong. The insides of buildings creep onto their façades without the deft touch of Richard Rogers. This strange sight is already a reality in Caracas, Venezuela: one of South America's tallest skyscrapers, the Torre de David, is home to over 4,000 squatters who took up residence in 2007 after construction had stalled – over a decade earlier, in 1994 – on the 45-storey building.

Above Earth, half a million very rich individuals live in the Elysium Torus, which has a depth of 2 km and a diameter of 40 km. Its five-spoke wheel design is based on the Stanford Torus, proposed in 1975, and the early space-station concepts of Wernher von Braun and Herman Potočnik. But Elysium, says Blomkamp, is 'Bel Air in space', replete with McMansions. To realize the habitat's interior, Syd Mead even superimposed a realistic Beverly Hills landscape atop his original hexagonal-grid plan, which was further developed and realized by VFX companies Image Engine Design and Whiskytree. The inclusion of McMansions – popularized in the United States and adopted by homebuyers in China – produces an absurd yet eye-catching design. As Ivey aptly notes: 'Money doesn't buy taste'. The proof of his words is in Bel Air itself, where many a classic modernist home has been torn down and replaced by a larger, gaudier McMansion.

According to Blomkamp, '*Elysium*'s meant to be a fork in the road.' His film shows a need for architects to exert a healthier influence on sociopolitical forces and to engage in a more public discourse.

Elysium is a massive space station orbiting above the Earth.

The floor of the living area merges seamlessly with that of the garden terrace.

Text **Masaaki Takahashi**
Photos **DYSK**

Double Negatives Architecture (DNA) is a group of architects, graphic designers, software programmers and one musician. It's led by Sota Ichikawa, an architect who has been in the industry since 1998. He designed a house for a resort in Nagohara, which is at the foot of the Yatsugatake Mountains, whose highest peak is 2,899 m.

The one-storey, one-room holiday home has a floor area of 85 m^2 and a steel frame. The exterior is covered in OSB (oriented strand board) that is finished in a coat of recently developed transparent paint, which is both waterproof and UV-resistant. The shape of the house – reminiscent of a snail shell – reflects DNA's aim to offer occupants a panoramic view of the woodland surroundings. About half the building is below

Plan

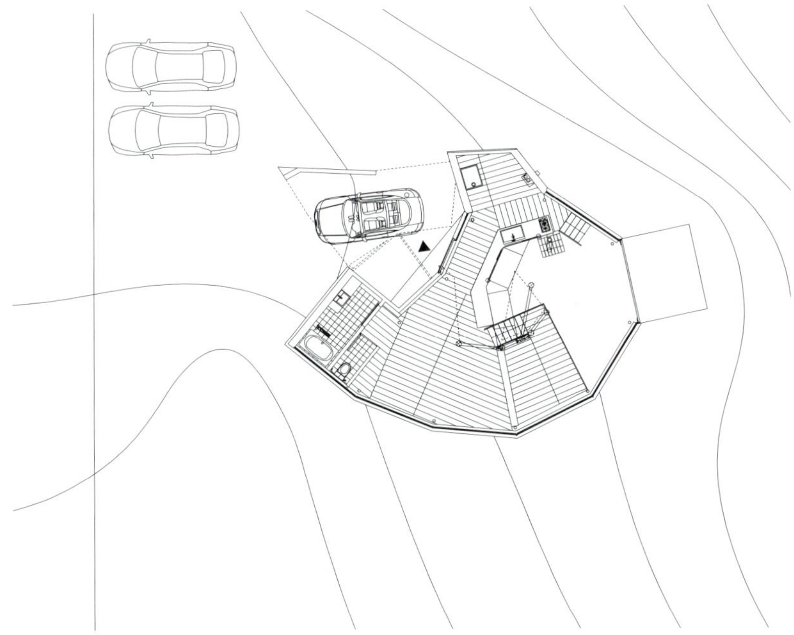

DNA continues the cycle of progress

ground level. The design incorporates various views of the outdoors, as well as interior sight-lines, enabling residents to fully appreciate the natural setting. An example is the view through the opening of a large wooden door that folds up. Another forest scene is revealed by means of an extremely low viewpoint.

The roof is a slab of reinforced in-situ concrete finished with mortar; the method used respects the rather complicated shape of the roof and the system of structural steel columns, which are close to one another. Ichikawa explains that he bases his designs mainly on the dimensions of the human body, objects and sites. A realized DNA project acts as a standard for dimensions used in later designs, continuing the cycle of progress.

doublenegatives.jp

Zaha Hadid **learns in Vienna**

Text **Pulane Mpotokwane**
Photos **Michael Hierner**

Zaha Hadid Architects recently completed a library and learning centre for the Vienna University for Economic and Business Administration. Hadid's extension is part of a master plan which includes five buildings that form a new block shaped by features in the existing urban fabric.

Horizontality emphasized on the façade and inside the building complements the neighbourhood's low- and medium-rise development. Exterior panelling made from glass fibre-reinforced concrete manufactured by the Rieder Group gives the landmark building its two-tone appearance.

The centre is characterized by two interlocking volumes: a public zone clad in black and a private zone in white. An internal walkway – articulated in glass on the façade – winds its way between and around the volumes, following a slanted zigzag trajectory. A glazed ceiling covering the walkway allows daylight to infiltrate the deep plan and, at the same time, outlines the building's main circulation artery.

The slanted zigzag motif influences virtually every element of the building. Hints of it can be seen in structural columns, light fixtures, handrails, furniture, mullions and bookcases. The zigzag is most prominent on the façade, where it delineates the glazed and concrete portions almost equally. These materials make the defining contour of the building visible both day and night.

Daylight is deliberately let into certain zones and kept out of others, illuminating reading rooms but avoiding bookshelves, casting a diffused glow over public atriums but sidestepping screening rooms. The black volume culminates in a viewing room illuminated by natural light – a space that overlooks Vienna and asserts the building as a new landmark for the city.

zaha-hadid.com

The project is situated opposite the popular Copenhagen summer hang out, Islands Brygge.

Text **Pulane Mpotokwane**
Photos **Urban Agency**

Urban Agency **and** JDS **make waves**

Dynamic, playful and responsive, Kalvebod Waves – designed by Urban Agency and JDS – is revamping Copenhagen's waterfront, one walkway at a time.

A pier sandwiched between a privatized waterfront area and a public waterway, Kalvebod Waves morphs from boulevard to boardwalk to skatepark, forming an urban playground that users can adapt to fulfil various uses through the year.

Henning Stüben of Urban Agency points out that a particularly interesting aspect of this urban-regeneration project is the way people have taken ownership of the space and become inventive in the ways they use it. They practise slacklining between the piles, skate down slopes and sunbathe on the steps. They even take afternoon naps on Kalvebod Waves, whose linearity and multiple levels ensure that 'you can have 200 people on there and still have privacy'.

The team built with materials known to function and weather well in industrial harbours. They used rough-textured concrete and saw-cut oak to minimize slippage, and stainless and galvanized steel for their resistance to rust. All materials were chosen for their durability in a maritime context, but also for their material properties and ability to encourage or enhance certain activities. 'Concrete is nice and warm in the sun and also good for skating,' says Stüben, 'whereas wood is softer and more comfortable to sit on in very hot or cold weather.'

Levels and dynamism are a big part of the project. A kayak slide on the boardwalk has been called 'too steep and dangerous' by local media, as it ends directly in the water and has no railing or other protective barrier to prevent people from falling in. (Copenhagen regulations do not require handrails on the waterfront.) That said, everyone can access Kalvebod Waves – just not all parts of it. Certain elements in the project were designed, as Stüben admits with a smile, 'for daredevils'.

The architects deliberately designed a place that 'provides the possibility for adventure but is still safe' and that encourages the creative use of urban space. 'We didn't want to over-programme it,' says Stüben. 'We wanted to make it the frame for unexpected things to happen.'

urban-agency.com
jdsa.eu

Valerie Van der Put **opens the windows of her mind**

Text **Pulane Mpotokwane**
Photos **Frederik Vercruysse**

Folding is the main formal strategy you've used here – the building folds over the landscape, floors fold into walls, and so on. What is the idea behind this?

VALERIE VAN DER PUT: Every design starts with a study of the distinctive qualities of the environment, as I try to find a way to blend the building into the character of place. Folding the floors to form a split-level house is a choice that is based on the landscape. The natural slope gives a feeling of protection and creates a boundary between public and private space. The asymmetric floor plan reinforces this concept by revealing a larger front and releasing a bigger garden in the back. It's nice that people don't know what they can expect from the outside. The higher up in the house you go, the more privacy there is. The building has a natural flow: no doors, one-way circulation, contact between floors, different perspectives, flexible zones, and few boundaries between inside and outside, so you feel connected to the environment.

You use sculptural furniture in your house and walls that are muted in colour and materiality. This relationship between architecture and objects is usually found in galleries. Would you say your house behaves like an exhibition space?

I must say I love spending time in museums, an activity that might have played a part in the design, but it's more that I see this house as a sculpture that doesn't need additions. So the objects stand in relation to the room without invading the harmony found there. Every space has its centrepieces, each of which looks different thanks to the white walls, while contrasting with the brutalism of the concrete and achieving a balance with the sand-coloured floor.

Is this your dream house?

I'm a creative person who likes to express my story instead of the history of houses. This house is a collection of thoughts and feelings to which I've given form. You can see through the windows of my mind. Space can be as complex as emotion, so there must be tension between the autonomy of the building and the idea of the builder. I took a very inspirational journey with this house – with the processes of designing and building it. When a place lets you feel peaceful and inspired, it is your dream home.

valerievanderput.be

Long Section

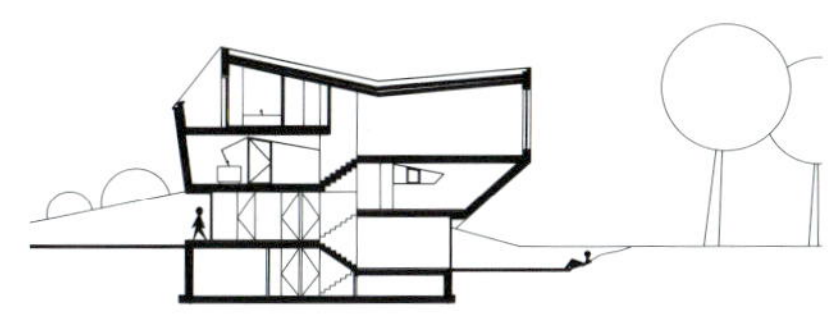

+ 2

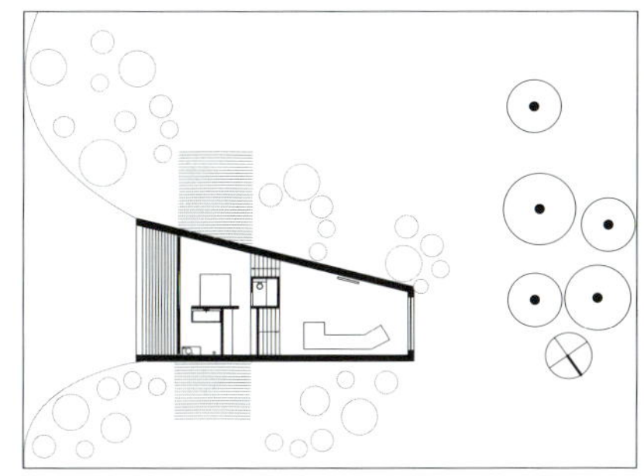

+ 1

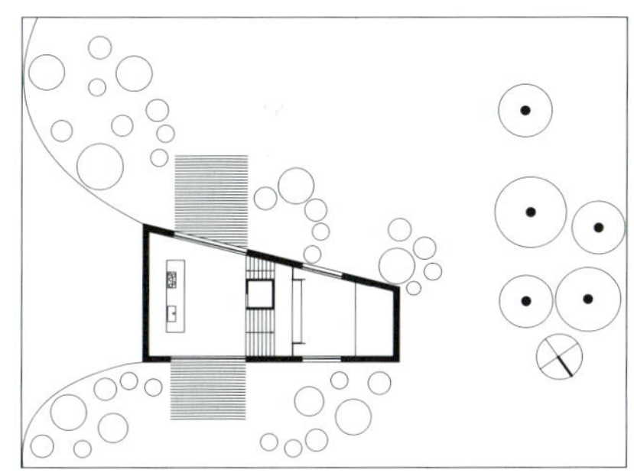

0

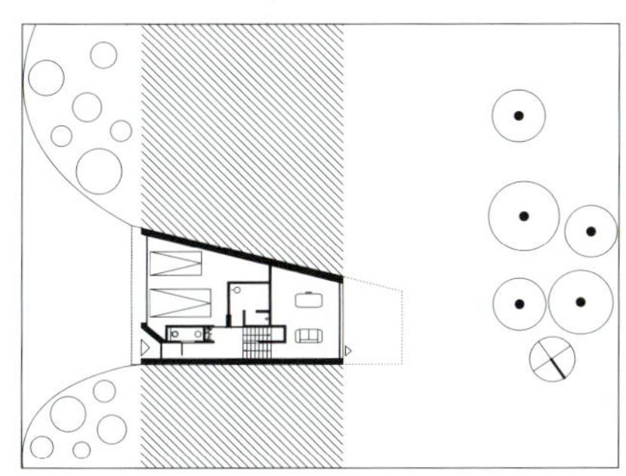

- 1

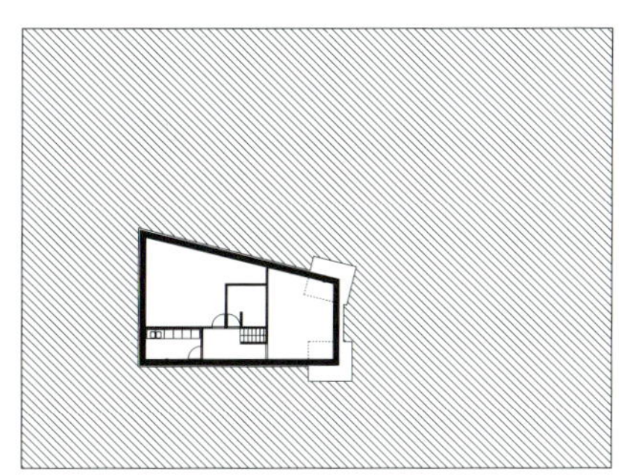

Shigeru Ban **redefines the office building in wood**

Text **Jane Szita**
Photos **Didier Boy de la Tour**

'It's not really up to me to get inspiration,' says Shigeru Ban. 'The client has a vision of what they want – so I go with that.' A modest statement from the architect of humble materials explains the origins of a curiously un-corporate office building he has just completed in Zurich for media group Tamedia. 'The owner wanted an office like a home,' he says, 'and as we were in Switzerland, I thought of all those wooden houses in the countryside.'

After that, it was wood all the way. 'I wanted to design a timber building – something that couldn't be done in steel. And I didn't want to use metal, or glue, or anything else. It had to be all wood.' Made of CNC-milled, untreated timber, the construction relies on a system of interlocking pieces, recalling traditional Japanese carpentry. Wooden posts are sandwiched between horizontal beams, and the framework is held in place by horizontal ovoid elements whose shape prevents them from rotating. Beams are left exposed, and a glass skin skims over the timber skeleton.

The structural system remains entirely visible, allowing it to be understood and giving the office building an unusually personal quality. The dominance of the natural material creates an atmosphere that Ban compares to that of 'a big log cabin'.

The carbon-neutral Tamedia building is seven storeys high, but Ban insists his technique can be used for much higher buildings, 'although fire regulations would mean that we would have to treat the wood'. The simplicity of the design, he adds, was unavoidable. 'Timber is a difficult material. You cannot weld it; you have to rely on geometry.'

shigerubanarchitects.com

Axonometric

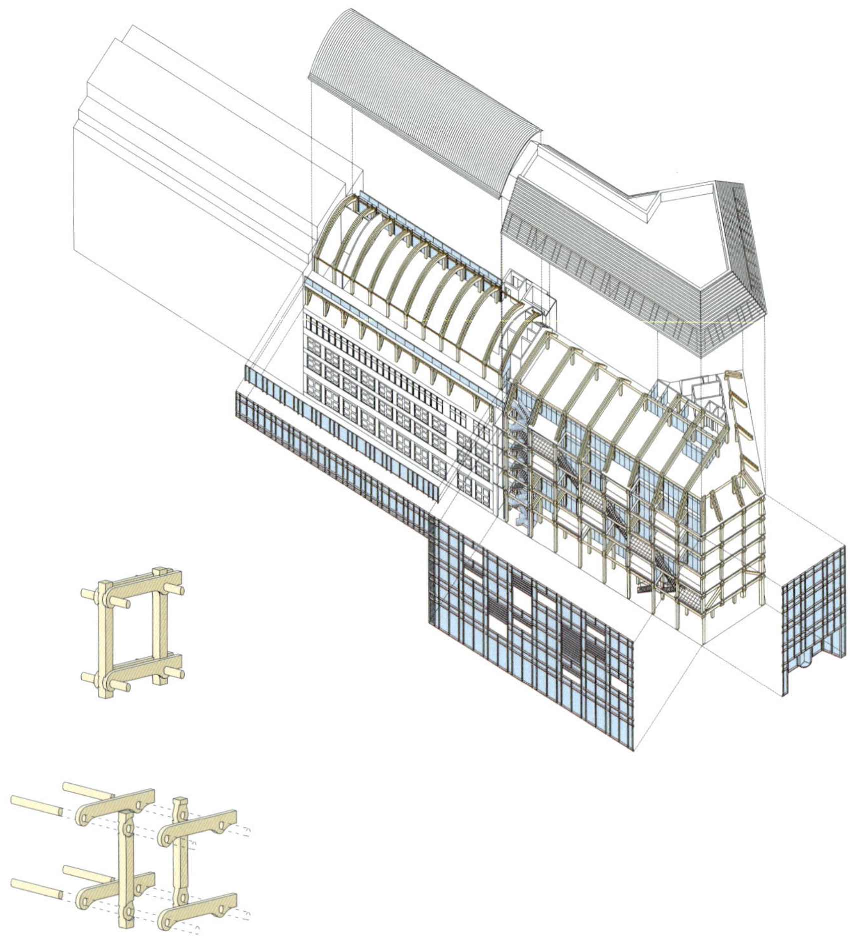

The intermediate space on the east façade is a thermal screen as well as an informal lounge area.

Mega Malls

Text and graphics **Theo Deutinger**

Thirty years ago, large-scale shopping malls were a strictly American phenomenon. It wasn't until the early 1990s that the development shifted to Asia, with the Philippines taking the lead, while the 2000s can be defined as 'the decade of the Chinese mega mall'. Currently, it looks as though the desire for huge retail complexes has moved to the Middle East.

Consumerism has hit Asia hard. Despite the poverty in this part of the world, mega malls – clean and, even more important, cool destinations – attract enough people to justify enormous investments, at least in terms of financial profit. In mall-saturated cities like Jakarta and vastly growing marketplaces like Istanbul, however, resistance to the development of shopping malls is on the rise. Jakarta's city council is reconsidering new projects, as so many of its existing malls occupy former parkland. Green Map Jakarta shows a decrease in the city's green areas from 35 per cent in 1985 to only 6 per cent today. On 28 May 2013, protesters in Istanbul launched a campaign against plans for replacing Taksim Gezi Park with a shopping mall. As of 10 September, these actions had cost the lives of seven people, primarily through police brutality.

But even the economic justification of mega malls is beginning to crumble. The mall boom in China, which has been going on for years and seems destined to continue – no less than half the world's 32 million m² of malls now under construction is in China, according to CBRE Group – has resulted in such a high vacancy rate that many malls have resorted to paying brands like H&M and Zara to move in. And no matter how fast China's middle class grows, the population of Chengdu, for example, cannot sustain four times as many malls as Los Angeles, a city of a similar size.

Most experts who are analysing China's present retail situation see a bubble that is about to burst. Plans for mega malls are already slowing down, and the world's largest shopping complex, the New South China Mall, is virtually unoccupied at the time of writing – and hasn't topped out since its completion eight years ago. Meanwhile, the emergence of the hype in the Middle East can be seen in temples of consumerism not only in the Emirates but also, surprisingly, in the cities of Iran.

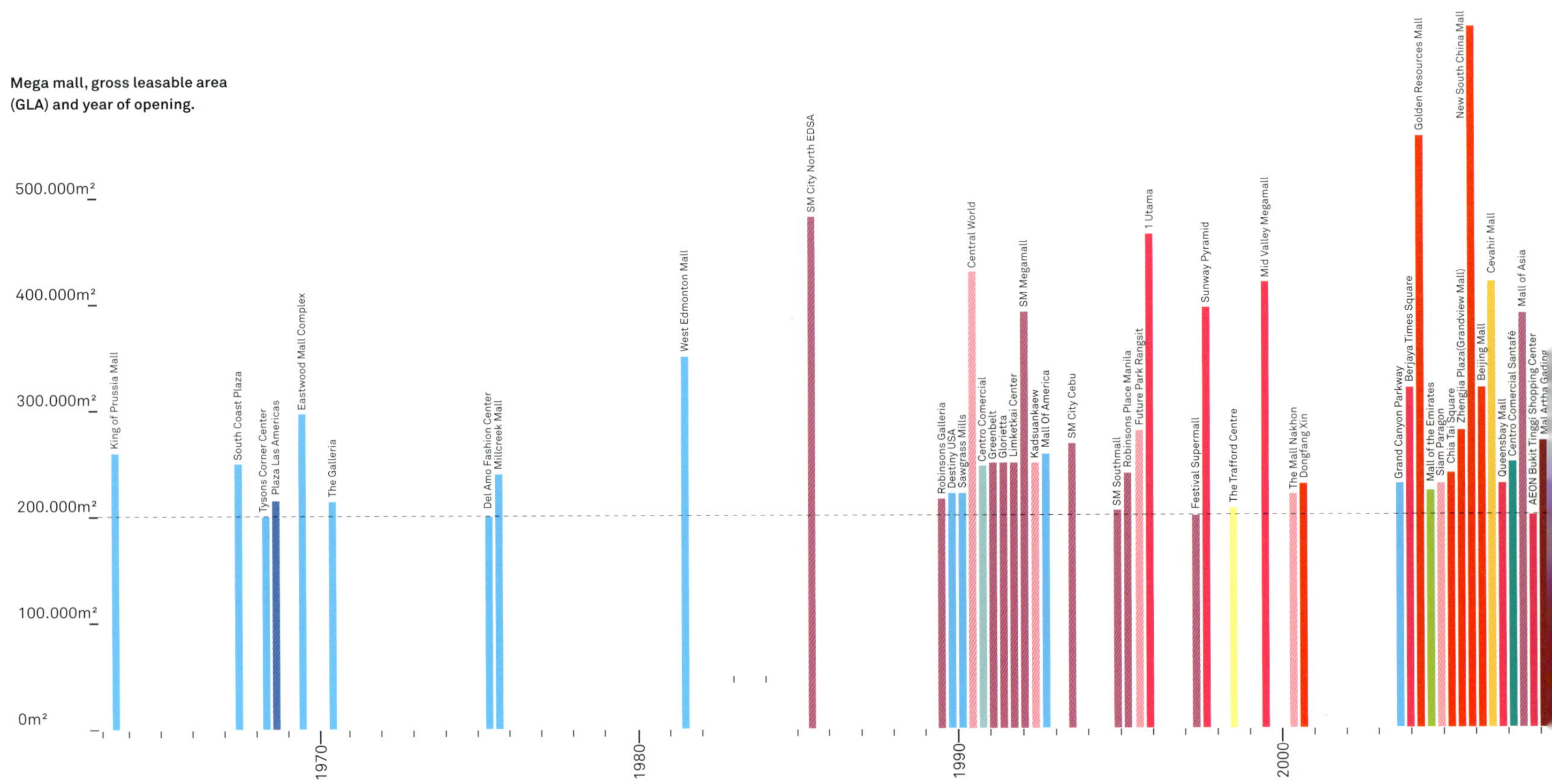

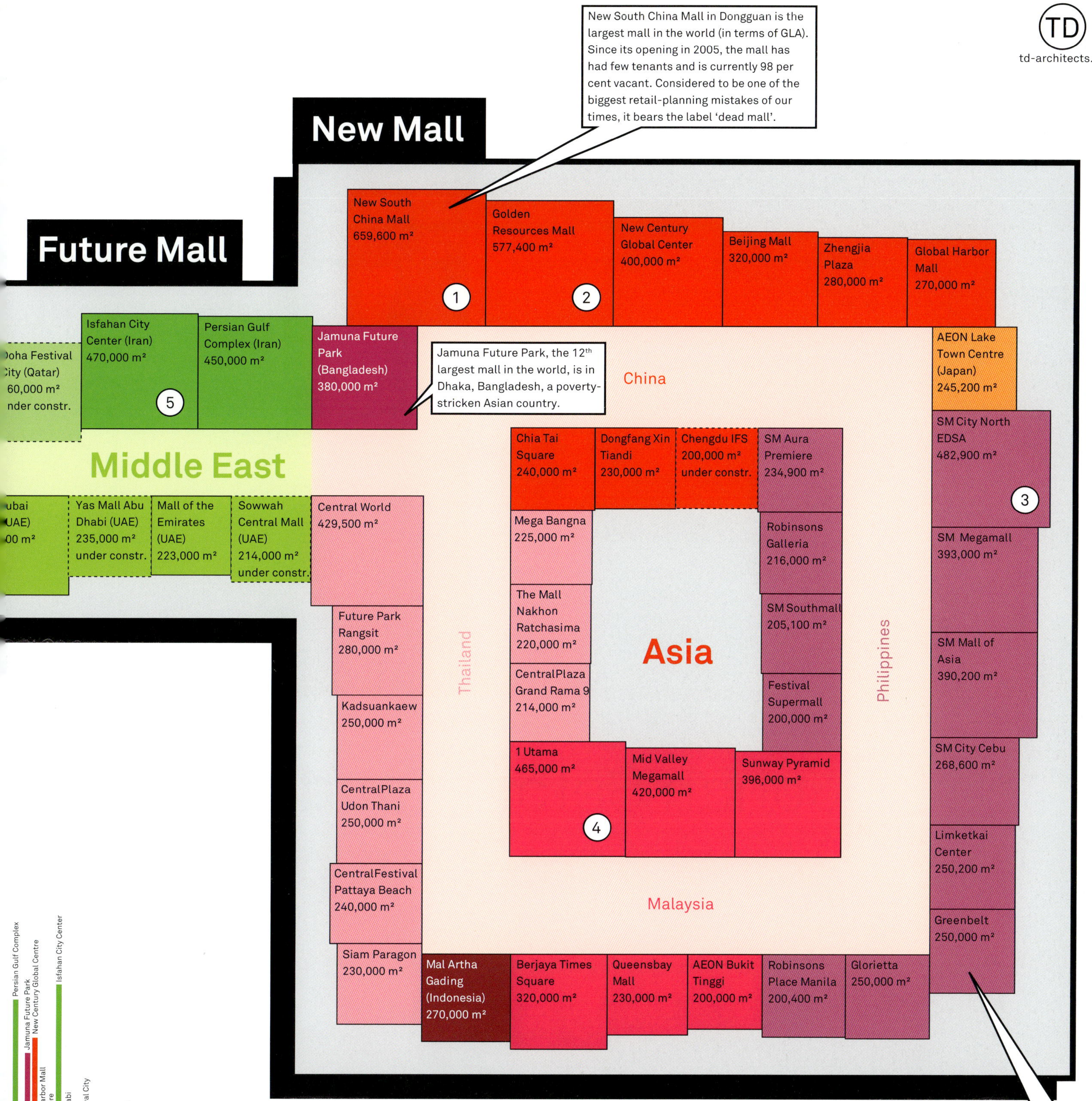

In the Philippines, half of all mega malls are owned by SM Prime Holdings, Inc., which operates 46 malls with a total gross floor area of 5.5 million m². In Asia, SM Prime is second only to CaptiaMalls Asia Ltd., with malls occupying a total gross floor area of approximately 8.6 million m².

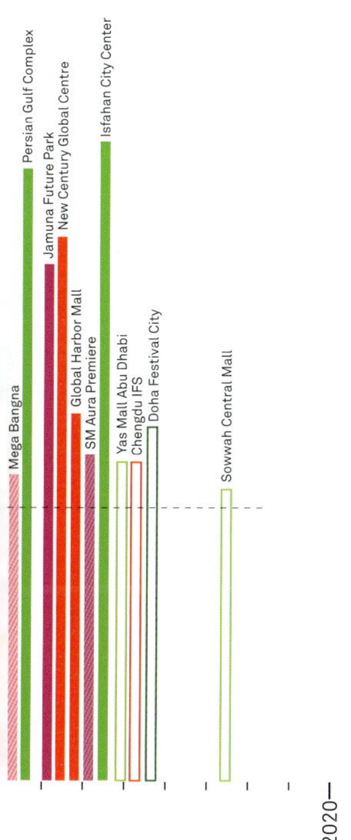

Philippines (12)	Canada (1)
United States (11)	Indonesia (1)
Thailand (9)	Colombia (1)
China (8)	Morocco (1)
Malaysia (6)	Brazil (1)
Iran (2)	Japan (1)
UAE (2)	Puerto Rico (1)
Turkey (1)	UK (1)
Bangladesh (1)	Spain (1)

① Top 5 Mega Malls

Mega malls are retail complexes with a gross leasable area (GLA) larger than 200,000 m².

Graphic sources
en.wikipedia.org
www.me-newswire.net
library.kiwix.org
en.classora.com

Text sources
thejakartaglobe.com
bloomberg.com
qz.com/118844/asias-mega-mall-boom-is-headed-toward-bust

Cross Section

Plan

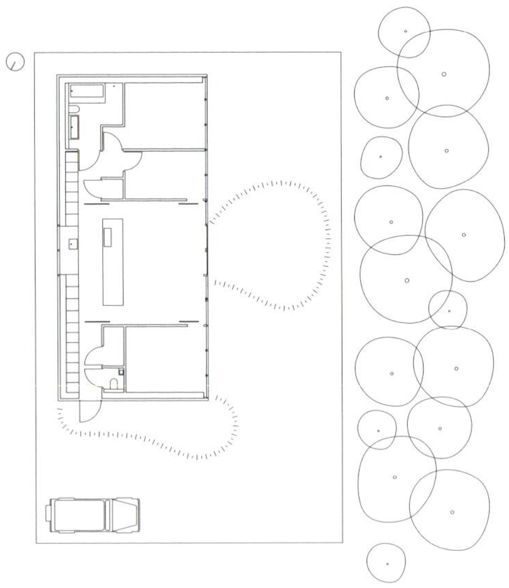

The house reflects its surroundings. The zinc dwelling on the left, designed by Klaas Kloosterboer of Made Architects, is called the Hive.

Johan Selbing **and** Anouk Vogel **parcel out privacy**

Text **Kirsten Hannema**
Photos **Jeroen Musch**

Mirror, mirror on the wall, which is the fairest house in De Eenvoud, an experimental housing project in the Dutch city of Almere? Answer: the Mirror House, designed by Johan Selbing and Anouk Vogel.

Following the completion of the Rubber House and the zinc Korf (Dutch for 'hive'), the Mirror House is the third residence to be built in the new neighbourhood, which is the fourth in a series of experimental housing estates in the city. The municipal initiative began in 2005 with a competition, Eenvoud (or 'simplicity'), aimed at promoting the design and construction of unusual homes. The brief: submit a simple yet intriguing idea for a house that can be built for €120,000.

What makes this glass pavilion – its design could hardly be simpler – so interesting are the contrasts it incorporates. The house presents itself as a minimalist sculpture, systematically avoiding such architectural elements as front door, roof gutters and window frames. At the same time, wrapped in reflective glass walls that melt into their surroundings, the rectangular volume appears to be one with the landscape. Seen from the outside, the house with its smooth-as-silk skin looks unbelievably crisp and cool. The view inside – where a spacious interior features custom-designed birch-ply cabinets, sliding walls and handy kitchen – transforms the observer's experience into something warm and friendly. The trump card of this 120-m^2 house, however, is the fact that people inside can see out, but people outside cannot see in. The reflective skin keeps indoor activities a secret, while ribbon fenestration concealed behind the main façade allows occupants to sneak a peek at the neighbours without being seen. In the meantime, a completely transparent rear wall offers a view of the woodland behind the house.

johanselbing.nl
anoukvogel.nl

Birch plywood has been used throughout the interior.

Plan

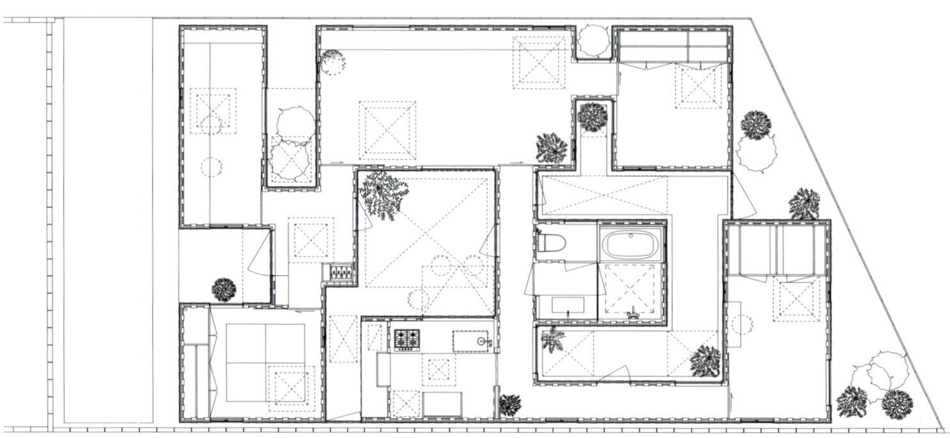

Atelier Tekuto **mixes interior and exterior**

Text **Cathelijne Nuijsink**
Photos **Toshihiro Sobajima**

What can you tell us about the site of your new project, Boundary House?

YASUHIRO YAMASHITA (Atelier Tekuto): The site is located in Chiba Prefecture, on the border between an urbanized residential area and farmland. To get there from Tokyo, you have to take a 40-minute train ride and then walk another 15 minutes from the station. It's a typical suburban site like many others in Japan. A lot of construction companies in such areas build and sell houses as if they were commodities, creating unattractive rows of cookie-cutter houses along the street. In this case, the contrast is great: unsightly homes right next to a scenic stretch of farmland. My intention was to treat this contrasting duality in a different way.

How did you envision the result?

Japan is a long, narrow archipelago that covers several climatic zones. We have four seasons, and we enjoy the gradual transition of nature from one season to another. The Japanese have an appreciation of conditions that are subtle and even ambiguous, rather than of clear distinctions between one thing and another. Ambiguity may have been considered negative in the 20th century, but today it should be seen as a positive quality, as the 21st century allows us to make flexible decisions within changing environments. In designing Boundary House, we envisioned a domestic life under a tarp-like structure that invites residents to feel nature and to move freely between inside and outside, using the design components of its mazelike composition. These include 16 skylights, potted plants, and complementary finishes for all interior and exterior walls and floors.

In what way does this house reflect your current ideas on design?

I am of the opinion that architecture should coexist quietly with nature, never opposing it. In the past, many houses were simply products or structures offering shelter from rain and wind. I am positive that a choice between these alternatives no longer applies to the current situation. Architecture and nature should be integrated. Both should be part of our daily life.

tekuto.com

Fuhrimann Hächler
towers over the Lake of Gods

Text **Pulane Mpotokwane**
Photos **Valentin Jeck**

Rowers call Rotsee the 'Lake of Gods'. Situated between rolling hills on the northern edge of Lucerne, Switzerland, the natural lake has virtually no currents and is protected from the wind, making it ideal for regattas. Rotsee was the site of the first international regatta in 1933 and has since been the preferred venue for Rowing World Cup series finals. It's easy to understand why rowing enthusiasts would be moved to call it a 'godsend'.

Fuhrimann Hächler recently completed a finish tower in the lake for the use of International Rowing Federation jurors, timekeepers and speakers. The design is contemporary and unassuming, yet has a classic quality that architect Gabrielle Hächler says gives it 'a certain elegance appropriate for the elite reputation of rowing and regattas'.

The architects used wood to construct the tower, which visually integrates the building into the landscape. Prefabricated pine panelling and concrete permitted them to stay within budget and to comply with time constraints. The pine was treated and will age slowly, eventually weathering to take on the grey tones of the concrete platform, rendering the two materials indistinguishable from each other.

The orthogonal composition of the tower contrasts with the organic forms of surrounding trees and its verticality with the horizontal contours of the landscape, while offsets between the building's three floors give the form energy and weightlessness, conveying a sporty spirit.

From outside, the tower draws attention to itself, as a landmark should. Inside, its minimally detailed interior fades into the foreground, drawing the eye to the windows and the stunning natural environment beyond. Long ribbon windows and short floor-to-ceiling heights further focus interior spaces on striking outdoor panoramas and accentuate the scenographic aspects of the building.

Windows are articulated with wooden shutters that slide, fold, and swing open and shut, creating a Cubist aesthetic and sense of vitality. Shutters also give the tower a dual character: dynamic, playful and inviting when open; sombre, solid and sculptural when closed. When open, they act as shading overhangs for windows and reflect ripples below, emphasizing the building's connection to water and motion.

afgh.ch

Long Section

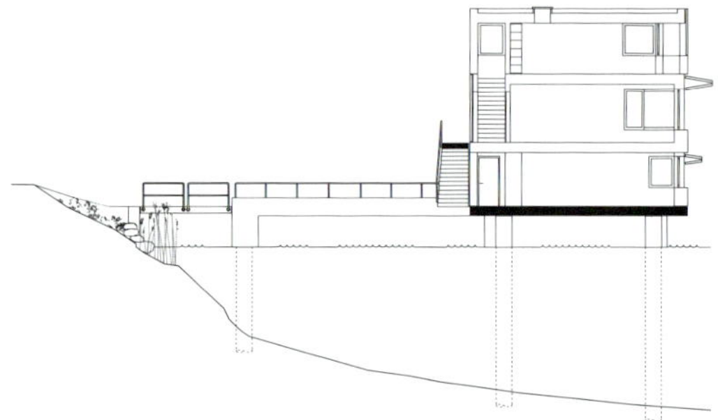

+2

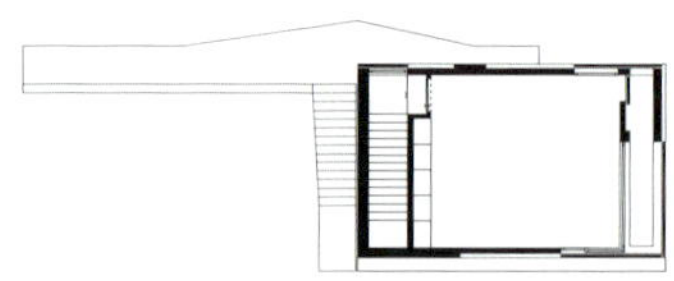

+1

0

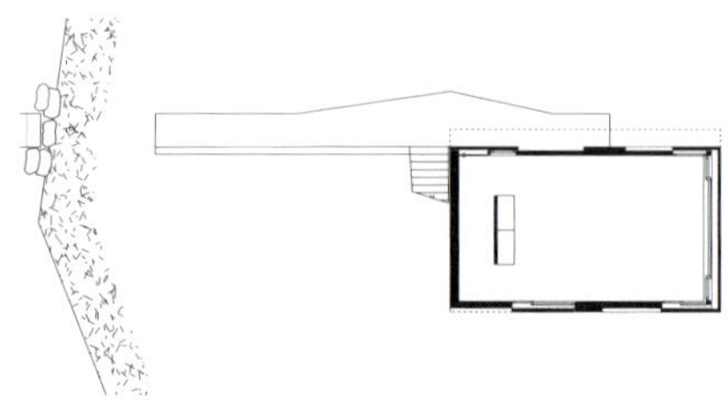

Finish Tower → Lucerne | Switzerland

F451 **brings the studio home**

Text **Jane Szita**
Photos **José Hevia**

Emerging enigmatically from the earth before branching into an irregularly faceted form, a house and studio for artist Lara Rios in Gijón, Spain, has an unusually dynamic relationship with its sloping site. The partly embedded building, by F451 Arquitectura, owes its intriguing shape to the architects' desire to make the most of the surrounding landscape, especially the nearby oak trees, but also to the rather complicated brief.

The client wanted 'a big atelier with natural light from the north, a house, a guest apartment, and a big garage and cellar', explains Toni Montes of F451 Arquitectura. What's more, 'all the programmes had to be autonomous and have their own independent access, yet be interrelated'.

The architects took these complex requirements as the starting point for what Montes calls 'an exploration of typological innovation', in which homely, domestic spaces coexist with a double-height studio designed to resemble 'an industrial shed'. Metal corrugated plate, exposed in the interior but insulated on the outside, references the industrial model, while walls made of honeycomb clay block increase thermal efficiency. Expanses of glass tie the house to views of the landscape at every opportunity or are angled to capture the desired northern light.

A grass-covered roof tops the guest apartment, smoothing the transition from buried to freestanding structure, while white-stucco planes signal the building's autonomy in the landscape. Both elements represent what Montes hopes is a 'symbiotic' relationship between structure and scenery.

f451arquitectura.com

Art, architecture and nature are rooted in the sloped terrain of an artist's house and studio.

Cross Section

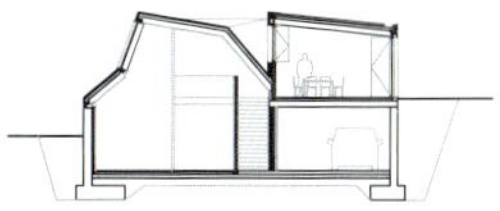

0

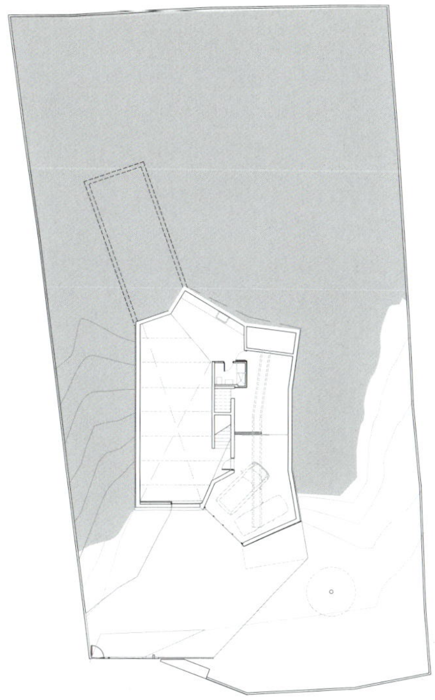

+ 1

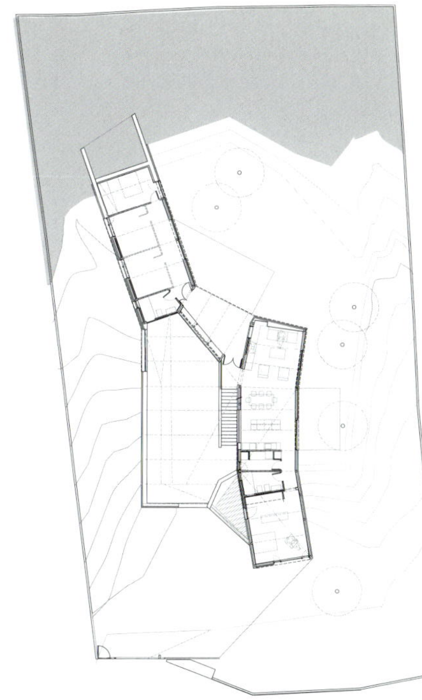

Tense **is on its guard**

Text **Ana Martins**
Photos **Filippo Poli**

A stern concrete shell discreetly wraps a three-storey house in Kallitechnoupolis, Greece. The project's most prominent feature, this sculptural carapace not only shields the building from two neighbouring properties but also frames inviting views of the distant hill and greenery. The design of the house – by Tilemachos Andrianopoulos, Kostas Mavros and Nestoras Kanellos of Athens-based studio Tense Architecture – features interior spaces that are open and bright while providing residents with maximum privacy. According to Andrianopoulos, 'The shell concept is a response to an urge for introversion triggered by the limited dimensions of the site.' Like the hillside on which it sits, the house expands from a narrow upper storey to wider floors below, creating stratified levels, each with floor-to-ceiling glazing that pulls in light while revealing the beauty of the surrounding landscape.

Discussing the house that Tense realized in Sykamino (*Mark* 44, page 148), the architects said that 'nothing is random', referring to a design process that is guided by the demands of the project itself, and not by a superimposed vision of architecture. Andrianopoulos sees the architect as a go-between who links the work with the forces that shape it: 'This process is nevertheless open to luck, or at least it should be. All true inventiveness is based on luck – possibilities for invention pop up all the time during the hot process' that leads to the design of a building. He says it's all about 'obedience to the natural force' that he calls 'luck'. An example of how luck influenced the house in Kallitechnoupolis? 'The curved partitions of the sleeping quarters,' he points out, 'emerged as a necessary counterpart to the external angularity of the building.'

tensearchitecture.net

Long Section

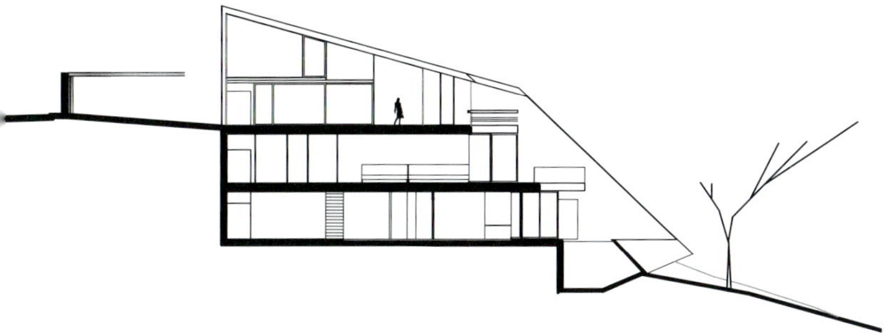

0

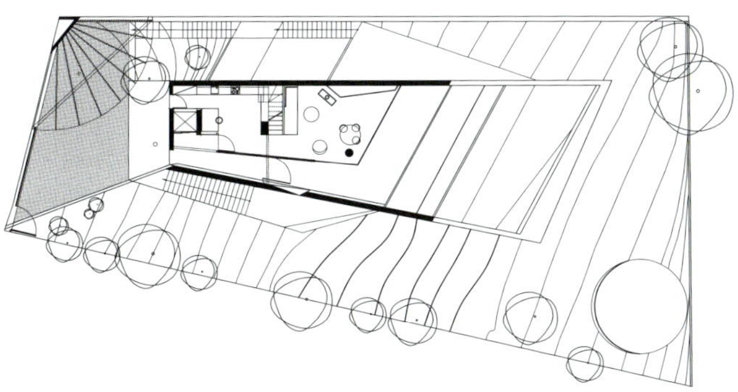

- 1

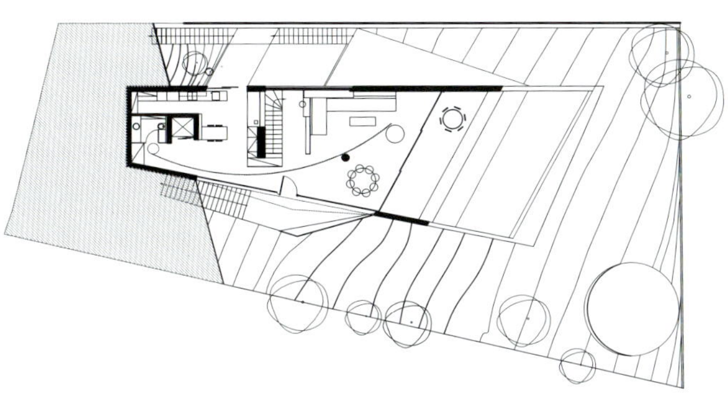

- 2

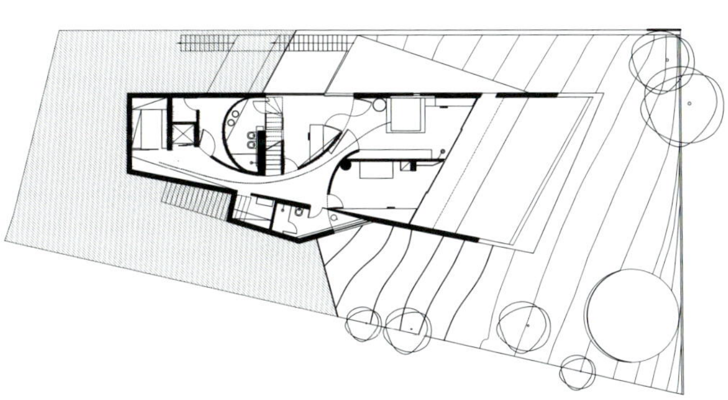

The clients can enjoy the landscape while being shielded from views.

Knight Architects **lifts and rolls**

Text **Pulane Mpotokwane**
Photos **Patrick Reynolds**

Maori culture – and a sensitivity to it – was one of Knight Architects' considerations while designing Hatea Bridge in Whangarei, New Zealand. The project is characterized by fabricated steel J beams, whose form was determined by the double lifting and rolling action of the bridge. These beams, which are the defining elements of the construction, mimic a fish-hook motif widely used in Maori iconography.

A rolling bascule bridge was chosen specifically for its double-action mechanism, which allows for fast opening and closing. This was an important aspect of a brief that asked for a bridge that would ease traffic congestion in the city centre, while also linking the Town Basin to William Fraser Memorial Park and creating connections to Whangarei Airport. The project is part of an urban regeneration and beautification scheme intended to mitigate the negative effects of industrial development along the Hatea waterfront.

Knight Architects used parametric modelling in the design-development stage of the project to find the most efficient form for the deck and minimize the amount of steel needed for construction. The result is a bridge with a slander profile and an energy-efficient, wind-resistant design. Decking on the outer edges of the bridge, which offers pedestrians a walkway, is made of permeable aluminium through which air can flow, reducing wind loads.

knightarchitects.co.uk

Long Section

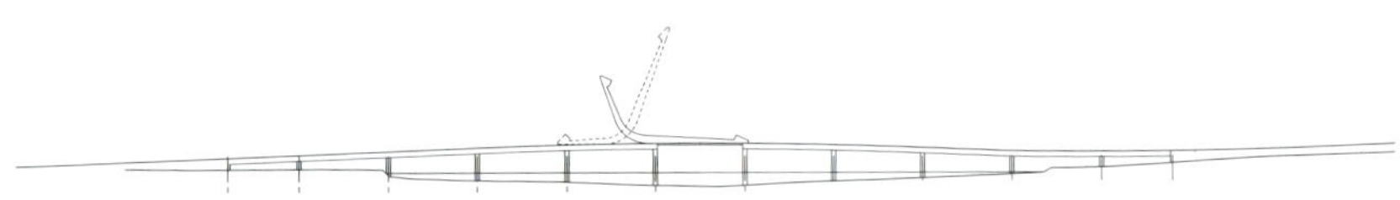

Plan

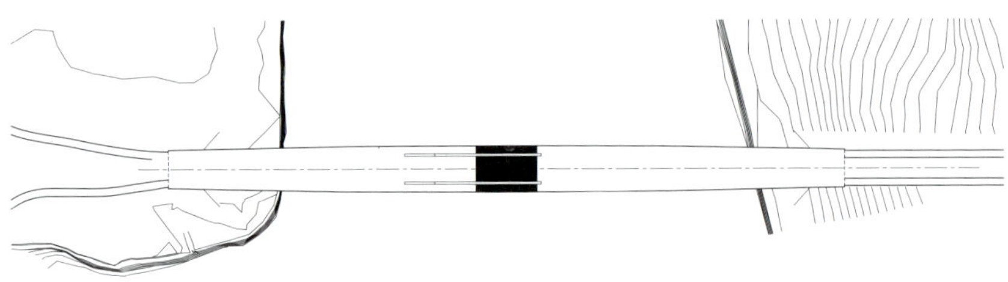

Bridge → Whangarei | New Zealand

Katsutoshi Sasaki **is inspired by a tree**

Text **Cathelijne Nuijsink**
Photos **Katsutoshi Sasaki + Associates**

KATSUTOSHI SASAKI: I changed my mind about architecture after the Great East Japan Earthquake of 2011. I began to believe that architecture should have a clear, primitive form. To be more concrete, I now believe that 'making a house' is the same as 'making family relations'.

This house was built for an engineer and his family. Before I started designing it, they had envisioned a home in which all parts of the interior interconnected to form a continuous space. Generally speaking, the layout of a contemporary Japanese house has one or more upper storeys and partition walls that interrupt the smooth flow that is possible in a home without such barriers. Here I was able to avoid internal divisions by basing my design on the concept of 'gathering underneath a tree'.

My metaphor for the design was the Japanese tradition of viewing cherry blossoms in full bloom each spring, when you see many families sitting under cherry trees looking happy and relaxed. I designed the house with this scene in mind. The main living space encircles a central wooden 'tree trunk'. Although the trunk prevents long sightlines, it also makes the nature of the space circulatory, allowing each member of the family to connect to the whole without feeling isolated. In my eyes, a spot beneath a tree, with moderate sunshine and a comfortable breeze, is a desirable place for a family to gather. I pictured that setting and made the house a place that combines light and shadow rather than a place with brightness everywhere.

sasaki-as.com

The lower, brighter part of the house accommodates living areas, and the wooden 'tree trunk' houses the bedrooms.

Long Section

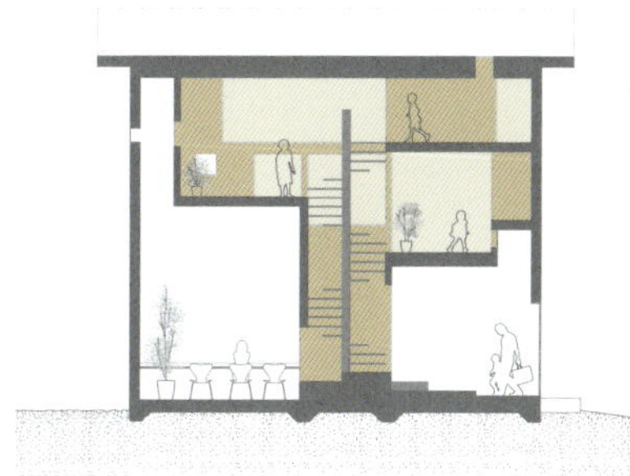

+ 2

+ 1

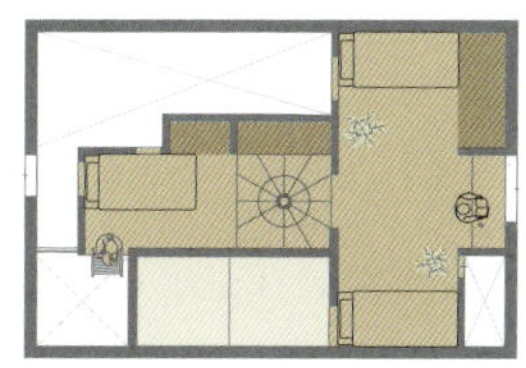

+ 0.5

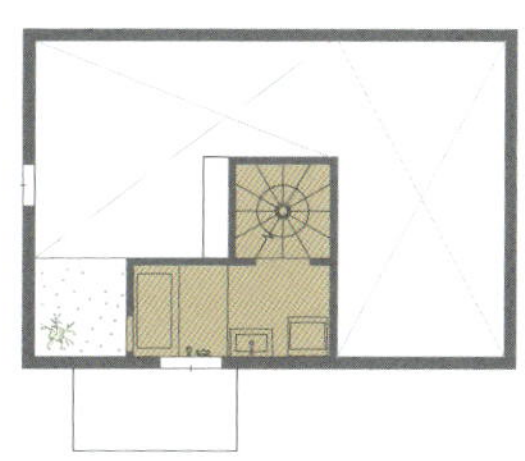

0

Perspective

Germany

What's Wrong with Germany?

When you take a cursory look at German architecture, you see reliable building methods, soundly established procedures and a strong construction industry. The cumulative result is architecture that may not produce the most exciting buildings, but they certainly appear to be solid, functional and sustainable. When you take a closer look, however, you may have to adjust that image. Germany, too, seems to have bit off more than it can chew when it comes to building projects plagued by unmanageable budgets, endlessly postponed completion dates and all sorts of political intrigue.

In this issue of *Mark*, we turn our attention to the three biggest planning headaches of the moment: Berlin Brandenburg Airport, the Elbe Philharmonic Hall in Hamburg and Stuttgart's central train station. High-profile architects are involved in all three projects, and all three are steeped in scandal. How did it get to this point? And what's going to happen now?

Photo Axel Schmies

Photo Marcus Bredt

Photo Armin Kilgus

Berlin

Perspective

Von Gerkan, Marg und Partner

Brandenburg Airport is completed, but a long way from opening.

Text
Falk Jaeger

Photos
Marcus Bredt

T

The new Berlin Brandenburg 'Willy Brand' airport, IATA code BER, was completed in May 2012. At least at first glance. There are buildings, and they have been fitted out and equipped with building services. Unfortunately, they are not yet ready for use. At the moment, people in the know are estimating that the airport will open in 2016. Five years later than planned and twice as expensive – it's a political and social scandal. The series of mistakes and negligence, particularly by politicians, that have led to this disaster are unparalleled.

↗ As a result of last-minute adjustments in the layout of the floors the rows of check-in counters in the departures hall had to be shortened.

↗ The baggage reclaim area looks empty and desolate.

↓ The landside of the airport terminal has an impressive canopy.

I. Original Plans

Originally, the airport was to be built by market parties. From an earlier tender in 1997, contractor Hochtief was chosen as the winner with a design by architecture firm von Gerkan, Marg und Partner. Because another competitor, contractor IVG, also successfully claimed the assignment, the result of the tender was declared invalid. However, in 2000 the battling parties united and formed a consortium. The clients, consisting of the Federal Republic of Germany and the federal states of Berlin and Brandenburg, were not willing to award the contract to the consortium, which now had no competition. In 2003 they abandoned the attempt to realize the project with market parties. 'We can do it cheaper ourselves,' said Klaus Wowereit, chairman of the Supervisory Board and mayor of Berlin. The Board decided to plan, build and run the airport itself, meaning under the responsibility of the government. (It subsequently turned out that the public airport company has been hopelessly overloaded with this project and that the costs are completely out of control; that is still the case today.)

In 2004 the 'Berlin Brandenburg International Project Company' (PG BBI), a General Partnership between von Gerkan, Marg und Partner Architekten (GMP), architecture firm JSK International and engineering consultants for building services Kruck, was awarded the contract for the design and planning permission application. After two failed tendering procedures for a chief contractor, the project tender was split up into seven parts.

A complete building schedule and fully detailed specifications were required for this purpose. Because only two offers came in, both far over the available budget, the time pressure increased. As a result, the PG BBI was asked to realize a successful tender for a smaller airport that was within the budget extremely quickly.

Uncertainty about the Scope

The specified objective of the client was to economize and remove 10 per cent of the required 220,000 m^2. This is where the airport's terminal space problems began. One special condition was the manoeuvre that, with retrospective effect, the division between passengers arriving from non-Schengen and Schengen countries (an EU requirement) had to be realized in the same volume.

The architects' recommendation to enlarge the building because of the required division of passengers rather than reducing its size was brushed aside because of the costs. One consequence of this decision was the extremely limited ceiling height on the ground floor and first floor, which led to significant problems later on in the process with the coordination and positioning of the building services. And every change in the design had a far-reaching impact on the costs and planning.

When the client included retail as well in the task in mid-2006, the designers indicated that there was no room for that. They proposed extending the main terminal hall in a northerly and southerly direction by one module (each by a little more than 43 m) and estimated the costs at 45 million euros. This proposal was also turned down on the grounds of cost – an expensive and wrong decision, as it later transpired. The further densification of the spatial arrangement while the volume remained the same increased the complexity of the task yet again.

At the same time as the changes were taking place in the programmatic requirements for the terminal, the piers grew from a reduced version to maximum dimensions. As a result, the floor surface increased from 200,000 to 340,000 m^2 and the costs from 490 million to 830 million Euros.

Expensive Changes

Afterwards, the design process progressed without problems for a while, until the client set up the Aviation (passenger handling and airlines) and Non-Aviation (trade, gastronomy, marketing and parking) departments. These departments each brought their own wishes into the project from mid-2006 (in other words, too late). The greatest problem with this was the new 'walk-through shop' retail concept, a shopping area through which all the passengers would be led directly after passing security control. Passengers who shop bring in more money, after all, than clients who only fly. For this reason, the entire departures hall in the terminal was thrown into confusion. This created more lucrative floor area on the airside, but also led to a reduction in the available space for check-in counters and handling capacity.

When the carcass of the underground train station was already in full progress, the railway authority became aware that one factor in the statistical calculations had not been taken into account: the collapse of columns in the event of a train derailment. The architects found a way to ensure the →

'The airport is completed and costs 30 million euros per month in maintenance'

← constructive integrity of the underground station by including the terminal situated above in the calculations at cross-project level. If they had not managed to do so, the train station would have had to be closed and demolished or filled up. However, the use of load-bearing walls in the terminal to strengthen the train station was accompanied by a limitation of the options for the course of the installations, which had negative consequences during later plan changes.

The haggling over where the double-decker A380 aircraft were to be stalled also had a serious impact. Because the A380 is a long-haul aircraft, it would have been logical to situate it in the non-Schengen area in the middle section of the terminal, but that position had been cut due to a lack of money and space. However, on the personal instructions of the mayor, the A380's position was reintroduced into the plans, but now in the Air Berlin area on the south side of the main pier, so outside the non-Schengen section. The architects called the necessary diversions a 'shift of floors', because the security controls, transfer stations, passenger streams and escape routes had to be changed on every floor, without adjusting the volume. Because the building preparations for the 'integration retail' project phase, which had already been issued with planning permission, were in full swing and the consequences of the 'shift of floors' phases still had to be included in the design, the changes were initially built without a permit, on the orders of the client.

The many changes in the design had considerable consequences for fire safety, which ultimately could no longer be controlled. The smoke flue in the 'marketplace' could serve as an example of the chaos the client caused. The scenarios for fire load were raised from 7 megawatt (in the design phases) to 36 megawatt (integration retail) and during the building phase even further to 42 megawatt (shift of floors). A load of 42 megawatt was used for calculations, because the shopping areas added later (with alcoholic drinks, perfume and tobacco) could burn down completely. Because the roof was already finished and the smoke flue ventilation had already been built in, extra ventilators and ducts had to be installed.

Lack of Control

With the stalling position of the A380 moved and the 'shift of floors', without paying any further attention to the impact on the costs and planning, a long series of confusing adaptations brought in by the clients began in 2009 without any control over planning and financial aspects. As a result, in early 2010 the directors of the airport company decided not to allow any more changes, so as not to put the intended moment of occupation in any more danger, at the very least. The state of the planning as of 29 February 2010 was from that moment on the only valid basis. But this resolution was also not kept.

In particular, the new EU directive of March 2010 about scanning liquids meant new adjustments because the German Federal Police need twice as much floor space for checking people as a result. Streams of passengers, escape routes and sanitary areas had to be shifted. The rows of check-in counters in the departure hall had to be shortened and the complete baggage transport from the check-in counters to the baggage sorting area had to be rebuilt.

The extra floor space required for this led to a further expansion of the terminal hall in the form of 'pavilions' added on either side. The opening date was put back, but the architects pointed out that this date was also only achievable if absolutely no more changes were allowed.

Between July 2010 and late March 2011, building activities came to a standstill as a result of the adjustments to the plans for the central section of the terminal. In the same period, the planners were hit by a tidal wave of 286 requests for adjustments and 201 commissions for changes. At the end of 2011, a third revision of the planning permission was necessary. The permit was granted in mid-November 2012, almost 6 months after the planned opening date. This goes to show that the approval authority was not willing to submit to the political pressure urging for a quick compromise. The airport company had expected to be able to reach an agreement on this, due to the pressure of time and the importance of the project.

Hectic Acceleration Measures

The numerous – badly considered – commissions that the clients awarded to the implementing companies in 2011 were mainly aimed at speeding up the building process, in an effort to stick with the opening date of 3 June 2012 after all. In this period, the clients and the project managers entered all sorts of individual agreements relating to the technical services directly with the parties carrying out the work, outside the appropriate planning procedure. As a result, there were communication problems between the planning and implementing companies themselves. Everyone built however it suited them. The project managers and building control had long since lost sight of the overall picture. Ultimately, the work carried out no longer matched the plan documentation on many points, including the documents belonging to the building application. As a result, the building no longer met the requirements of the planning permission originally granted. A valid, well-considered and legal plan for fire safety was lacking up until the planned opening in June 2012, and was only made available to the builders, checked and released for implementation in November 2012. Nevertheless, in the test phase the fireproofing failed.

'Operating Permit before Completion' Failed

The plan was to open the airport prematurely with an 'operating permit before completion'. In addition, the automatic management of the fire installations would be replaced with manual operation by employees. The approval authority at the relevant district administration, Dahme-Spreewald, rejected this solution. We now know that, in addition to the IT →

Long Section

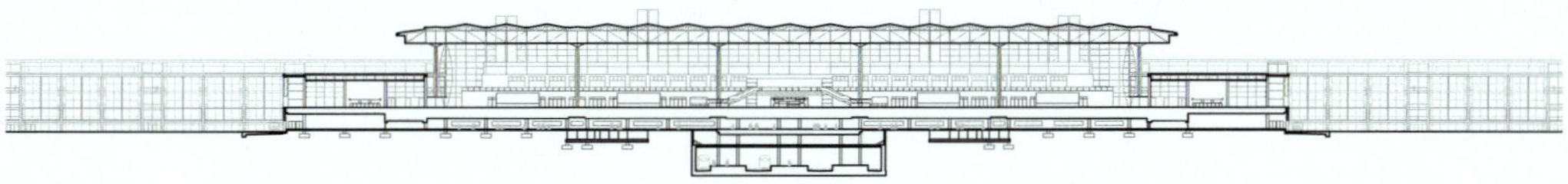

Plan

Departure level

01 Melli-Beese-Ring
02 Check-in
03 Passport control
04 Departure lounges
05 Piers

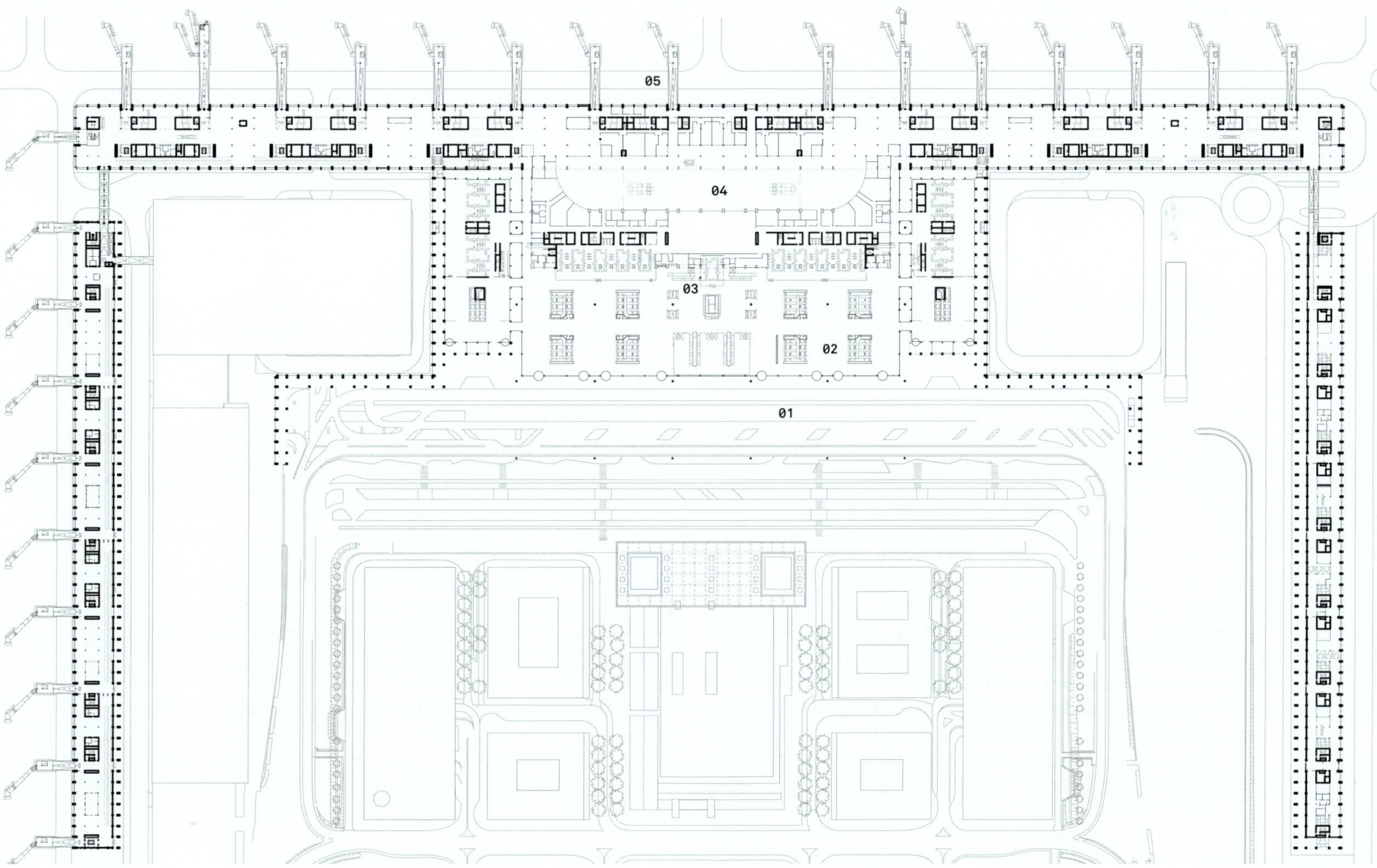

‘The airport was completed five years later than planned and is twice as expensive’

← connections for the fire installation and the freight handling, Customs was not ready to open either, due to a LAN that was still instable. The emergency power facilities for various departments were not yet functioning and the parking garages still had to be tested. The airport was not ready to be taken into commission in any way whatsoever.

Project Management and Building Control Fall Short

When the opening date of 6 June 2012 failed, which was announced in the media with an immense clarion call, the Supervisory Board (led by politicians) made the next wrong decision and this one proved fatal. Almost all the problems, errors and alleged scandals were publicly blamed on the architects. This is hardly surprising, because many people, including those politically and officially responsible, did not understand the difference in this complex matter between construction supervision, building inspection, building management, project management and coordination. That also holds true for the Supervisory Board with the mayor of Berlin and the prime minister of the Federal State of Brandenburg. Advised by the chairman of the airport company, they falsely blamed the PG BBI instead of the project management of the airport company itself as chiefly responsible. The PG BBI, with its 300 architects and engineers, was subsequently dismissed, and with them the collective memory of an extremely complex building enterprise. The only people who had really failed were the people from project management and building control, but they remained in place.

II. Current State of Affairs

The airport buildings, now completed, cost 30 million euros per month in maintenance. Not yet completed are the extremely complex fire installations and IT systems, which is why the airport has still not been given permission to open. The postponement of the opening in June 2012 to an unknown date in the future and the construction stop have meant that the agreements reached with the implementing companies no longer have a foundation. The companies have pulled their staff from the building site and employed them elsewhere. Many companies have made further involvement in BER airport dependent on payment of the commissions granted underhandedly during the acceleration phase. These must now be examined carefully. In addition, for a possible restart of work the companies require faultless planning documents, which can only be achieved with a great deal of difficulty in a survey of the undocumented building situation. The situation is further complicated by the on-the-spot dismissal of PG BBI, and with it the know-how of the planners, on 23 May 2012.

The current state of affairs makes it almost impossible to enter into agreements with planning firms and building businesses that can guarantee a certain delivery deadline. The only employment terms possible are expensive and based on hourly rates. The clients have no means of exercising any power whatsoever.

In mid-January 2013 Rainer Schwarz, the incompetent chairman of the airport company’s Executive Board, was finally dismissed, after he had long enjoyed the support of the Supervisory Board. His successor Hartmut Mehdorn, former head of the German Railways and manager of Air Berlin, has put together a ‘Sprint Team’ that brings the architects from GMP on board again. The survey of the existing state of building work has already taken 15 months and is a futile attempt to understand and chart the installations that were constructed in a hectic, indiscriminate way in 2012 and the many kilometres of ducting.

III. What Now?

New planning teams are now trying to install stable fire and IT systems while utilizing as much of the existing hardware as possible. The new management at the airport is attempting to induce the numerous building companies, through a combination of demands and legal hullabaloo, to enter into new agreements and to commit cooperatively to the delivery of the airport, instead of initiating a shower of court cases. It’s an expensive business and that gives the companies serious bargaining power. For instance, the decision was taken for the fire installations to adapt the problematic interface between the Bosch and Siemens systems in favour of Siemens, which has led to claims from both companies.

It is still uncertain at what time all the companies will be back at work and when the airport company will once again have a firm grasp on the building site. The same is true for how much longer the survey of the state of the building work and the test phase will take.

In mid-September the chairman of the Executive Board cancelled the publication of the opening date, announced for 25 October. To be quite clear: the announcement of the publication, not the publication itself.

2015? 2016? The airport company has failed in every respect as client and project management. The political Supervisory Board, which was apparently not capable of keeping control of the airport company, has delivered a botch-job. The Executive Board was dismissed (too late). The politicians, whose negligence has cost more than a billion euros of public money, are still in their functions. The Berliners take it all with a fatalistic attitude or with humour, depending on their temperament. ←

gmp-architekten.com

Black Box BER: A Review

Text **Florian Heilmeyer**

It must bother Meinhard von Gerkan to no end that for years all mess-ups and failures on the construction site of Berlin's new airport have been connected to his name. After all, Von Gerkan, Marg und Partner (GMP) is one of Germany's most renowned architecture firms, and its very first project, Berlin-Tegel, is one of the world's most beautiful airports.

In 2012, problems among architects, contractors and project managers culminated in a full-blown crisis that led to the architects' termination. Von Gerkan decided to take a step that's very unusual for an architect. He wrote a book, *Black Box BER*, in which he outlined everything that went wrong and why, from his point of view, on 160 pages.

Take, for example, the horror story about escalators that were three steps too short. It's a picture that instantly hit the press and made people laugh: escalators that ended directly in front of three concrete steps. Were these Hamburg-based architects too stupid to plan and build an escalator for the Berlin-Brandenburg airport? In his book, Von Gerkan finally got to tell his side of the story. 'Originally, the square in front of the airport train station was supposed to be overbuilt. The clients scrapped that plan, but the station's basic structure was already in place and the escalators were already ordered.' It's an argumentation that runs through the whole book – the management was overwhelmed; the deadlines, set by politicians, were 'a fairy tale' from the outset; and the client was never there.

Architects are service providers and, as such, often overly cautious. To their clients, they display a generally uncompromising, vassal-like loyalty. If this is the rule, Von Gerkan is an exception. At 78, the architect feels no need to cosy up to anybody, but he does have a reputation to defend. His well-written, amusing and convincingly illustrated book is the polemic of an angry old man and reads a bit like Stéphane Hessel's *Time for Outrage*, but this is the indignation of an architect. Von Gerkan relentlessly lists mistakes and failures, while telling stories and anecdotes, seemingly aiming his barbs at contemporary culture in general – a culture expressed in part by architecture.

He writes about the international decline of quality, using architecture as an example. Private investors are interested only in accruing maximum profits with minimum expenditures, an ambition that leads to 'banal architecture' and makes the latest Berlin airport a 'shopping mall with an adjacent airport'. Public clients don't fare any better; they are simply a 'large abstract presence' that 'curses or repudiates itself and doesn't take on any personal responsibility', especially in the case of large-scale projects. This explains the Berlin airport management's 'resistance to dialogue'. Changes were not 'discussed' but 'ordered'. According to Von Gerkan, there was 'no concept, only insatiable desire'. He claims that good architecture is no longer possible on large projects, thanks to commerce, consumption and misplaced responsibility. In the end, the Berlin-Brandenburg airport project collapsed in the face of 487 changes and simultaneous deadline pressure.

Even if much of what Von Gerkan writes is correct, what is blatantly missing in his book is real self-criticism. He considers himself a victim, stuck between absurd and contradictory demands. Clearly his black box is not a neutral recording device containing data meant to analyse a disaster after the fact. Only once does he mention that in hindsight he sees it as a failure that problems were not made public earlier – an easy out, especially in conjunction with a comment about his employees (not Von Gerkan himself) discovering that 'protocols and timelines were sugar-coated', which implies that his public clients and their 'committee' intentionally lied about the reality of the situation. This is a hard and pointed accusation that makes the architects – if one reads between the lines – complicit in the deceit that ultimately cost German taxpayers millions of euros.

Thus the main question raised by this book is: How on earth can we change a disastrous, decades-in-the-making situation that sees public building projects in Germany intentionally 'embellished' in terms of both cost and scheduling? All parties involved have benefited from this system far too long – except the taxpayer, of course, who's forced to pick up the tab. Everyone else, including the architects, is paid for the necessary changes in plans, just as Von Gerkan was paid for what had to be altered at Berlin-Brandenburg, a fact we don't read much about in his book.

This dovetails into another issue: Von Gerkan recently tried to revise the book, as GMP has now resumed work on the project and he wanted to amend the text. The publishing house, Quadriga Verlag, rejected his request, however, and printed the book as is, contending that the construction site will be a topic for years to come, and you can't update a book with every change. It almost looks as if Quadriga is the only one that's drawn the right conclusions in the endless series of mishaps plaguing Berlin-Brandenburg. ←

Meinhard von Gerkan, *Black Box BER: Vom Flughafen Berlin-Brandenburg und anderen Großbaustellen. Wie Deutschland seine Zukunft verbaut*, Quadriga Verlag, 160 pages, €14.99, ISBN 978-3-869-95060-0

Hamburg

The Elbe Philharmonic Hall turns out to be over ten times more expensive than originally calculated, leaving Hamburg with high hopes of a Sydney Opera House effect.

Text
Anneke Bokern

The Elbe Philharmonic Hall in September 2013.
Photo Axel Schmies

F

From €77 to €789 million in just ten years: the increase in the cost of building the Elbe Philharmonic Hall in Hamburg boggles the mind. Luckily, the building itself, by Herzog & de Meuron, promises to be just as mind-boggling upon completion. Designed to house three concert halls, a hotel and luxury apartments, it sits atop an old warehouse in the city's prestigious new HafenCity area. With its ornamental glass façade, wedge-shaped footprint and dramatically undulating roof, the building looks like a sci-fi ocean liner leaving the harbour. In fact, it's a modern-day version of the 'City Crown', the iconic mega-building utopia developed by German expressionist architects in the 1920s. And once it's finished, the complex will accommodate concert halls anticipated to be among the top ten in the world.

At the moment, however, hardly anyone seems to be interested in the architecture of the Elbe Philharmonic Hall – the current buzz is all about the price tag. No wonder, considering that the building will cost at least ten times more than originally calculated and is scheduled to open seven years later than planned. Budget overrun is too mild a term for this explosion, for which all parties involved – politicians, contractor, architects, investor – put the blame on someone other than themselves.

Generally speaking, Germans love buildings that boast intricate technical solutions and an impressive appearance, and many have developed a complicated love-hate relationship with the Elbe Philharmonic Hall. The media bash it, everybody complains about it, yet going to see it is a must. The exterior of the building is as good as finished and draws crowds every day, and a guided tour through the site has to be booked two months in advance. Everybody wants to see Hamburg's biggest money pit – even in its unfinished state.

→ An 82-m-long cave-like escalator leads to the public plaza on the roof of the old warehouse. Photo, July 2013.
Photo Oliver Heissner

→ Stairs leading to one of the smaller auditoriums, under construction.
Photo Oliver Heissner

↙ The foyer of the main auditorium, under construction.
Photo Oliver Heissner

I. Original Plans

The Elbe Philharmonic Hall is located on Kaiserhöft, the tip of a peninsula at the western end of HafenCity, a revitalized harbour area. The site was originally occupied by the Kaiserspeicher, a warehouse built in 1875, heavily damaged in the Second World War, demolished in 1963, and replaced by Kaispeicher A, a warehouse (for cocoa, tea and tobacco) designed by architect Werner Kallmorgen. It lost its function altogether when harbour activities relocated in the 1970s. In 2001, when conversion plans for HafenCity were already in full swing, an international competition was held for an office building to be erected in its place. The winner was Amsterdam-based Benthem Crouwel, whose proposal featured a 100-m-high glass tower next to a new triangular building, replicating the shape and dimensions of Kaispeicher A. Two years later, though, the investor still hadn't found tenants for the offices and the city council cancelled the project.

By then, new project developer Alexander Gérard had already entered the scene with another idea. In October 2001 he presented his plans for a concert hall to be placed on top of the old warehouse. At first the senate of Hamburg wasn't too enthusiastic, but in June 2003 Gérard produced the first designs by Herzog & de Meuron, and six months later the senate agreed to build the Elbe Philharmonic Hall. Herzog & de Meuron received the commission without having to face competition.

The original plans showed a new glass extension rising from the nearly windowless, wedge-shaped warehouse. The contrast could not have been greater: heavy, closed, brick walls below and light, transparent, glass walls on top. The Elbe Philharmonic Hall is a dramatic cherry on a minimalist cake. Inside is a vineyard-style concert hall with a central stage around which seats rise in serried rows. Its tentlike roof is echoed in the building's exterior silhouette. Besides the concert hall, the building includes a hotel on the 9th to 20th floors and 45 luxury apartments on the upper floors. Its highest point is 110 m and its lowest 30 m. All functions are accessible from a public plaza on the roof of the old warehouse, which is accessed via an 82-m-long cave-like escalator and divided into zones under large vaults. Recesses cut into the building above the plaza provide glimpses of the foyers, but even more impressive is the grand view of Hamburg.

No less spectacular than the overall shape of the building is its façade, consisting of more than 1,000 warped-glass panels printed with a sunscreen grid pattern (*Mark* 35, pages 206-209). The hotel section has wave-shaped ventilation hatches, and the apartments have horseshoe-shaped balconies. Each glass panel is unique, and the varying density of the grid is based on the use of the room behind the panel. Above a certain height, the south and west façades have a denser printed image, which allows the radar of incoming ships to locate the building.

At 110 m, the Elbe Philharmonic Hall will be the tallest inhabited structure in Hamburg. The main objective of the project goes beyond height, however, and envisions a building with the infamous Bilbao effect or, in this case, more of a Sydney Opera House effect. Apparently, the city's desire for a landmark icon was so strong that money could almost be ignored. When the foundation stone was laid in April 2007, the building was scheduled for completion in 2010, and cost estimates had already risen to €241 million.

Today, over six years later, the big question is: from €77 to €789 million – how the hell did that happen? Well, it's a long and complicated story, and nobody seems to have a good explanation. A parliamentary investigating committee that started looking into the matter in May 2010 has little to show for its trouble. Without a sense of objectivity, all you have are a diversity of opinions and lots of people pointing fingers at one another.

In 2004 – three years before the foundation stone was laid – Hamburg's joint venture with the project developer failed, and the city took over the project. The coming years saw several important changes made to the plan. Instead of one concert hall, there will now be three halls with 2,150, 550 and 170 seats. The hotel has been enlarged to include a wellness area and a glazed terrace. Even more important is the removal of the entire core of the old warehouse – left untouched in the original plans – in order to accommodate a parking garage for 540 vehicles and a music studio. →

Aerial photo, August 2012. The exterior of the building is as good as finished.
Photo Axel Schmies

← Of Kallmorgen's Kaispeicher A, considered by many to be one of Hamburg's more important post-war modernist buildings, only the listed façade has been preserved. Because the foundations were not strong enough to support the extra weight of the extended programme, they had to be reinforced. In addition to the 1,111 existing piles, another 650 steel piles were driven into the River Elbe sludge. To keep the outer walls from collapsing when the core was removed, they had to be supported by eight 340-m-long steel belts, resulting in even more costs. During the topping-out ceremony in May 2010, protesters distributed fake €350 million banknotes: the price tag attached to the building at that time.

All changes – purportedly over 3,500 modifications of consequence – required numerous revisions of the construction plans. At one point, contractor Hochtief and Herzog & de Meuron started to accuse each other of not delivering plans on time or even of withholding them on purpose. In 2009 the contractor questioned the static calculation of the roof, making extra controls and alterations necessary, and when measures to ensure fire safety had to be revised in October 2011, construction was postponed. Meanwhile, the money meter kept ticking, and more and more voices, especially from the German media, called for a cancellation of the entire project. In November 2012 the contractor finally resumed work and agreed to lower the new roof onto the warehouse. At the same time, Herzog & de Meuron presented large styrofoam models of the Elbe Philharmonic Hall at the Venice Biennale, accompanied by walls covered in newspaper articles about the project. Nothing could have made the controversy more tangible. By then, the opening date had been moved to summer 2015, and cost estimates had increased to €476 million.

II. Current State of Affairs

Last April the city of Hamburg and contractor Hochtief signed a revised contract. Hochtief has committed to finish the building by October 2016 for a fixed price of €575 million, resulting in total costs of €789 million. The opening is scheduled for spring 2017.

III. What Now?

So what's really caused all this trouble? Was the idea of placing a concert hall on top of a warehouse doomed to struggle from the start? Has the project been overcomplicated by adding too many extras? Has the contractor cheated taxpayers by asking for too much money? Have the investors messed up? Or the project management? Are Herzog & de Meuron and their overambitious design to blame? Who knows? In an interview with news magazine *Der Spiegel*, Pierre de Meuron recently compared the design of the Elbe Philharmonic Hall to the design of a cup: 'They initially said it had to be white and somehow contain tea. That was roughly what was stated in the call for bids at the time. But no one said how big it should be, that it also needed a saucer and possibly even a spoon. And if all that isn't in the specifications, you cannot, with a clear conscience, set a price or agree to fixed schedules.'

The only thing that's certain is that this project is long past the point of no return and has become too big to fail. Hamburg will get its iconic landmark at whatever cost. After all, Sydney Opera House cost 14 times more than the initial estimate. And who cares about that today? ←

herzogdemeuron.com

Rendering of the main auditorium.

Rendering of the foyer that encircles the main auditorium.

Rendering of the plaza, a public space under the main auditorium.

‘Germans have a complicated love-hate relationship with the Elbe Philharmonic Hall’

+10

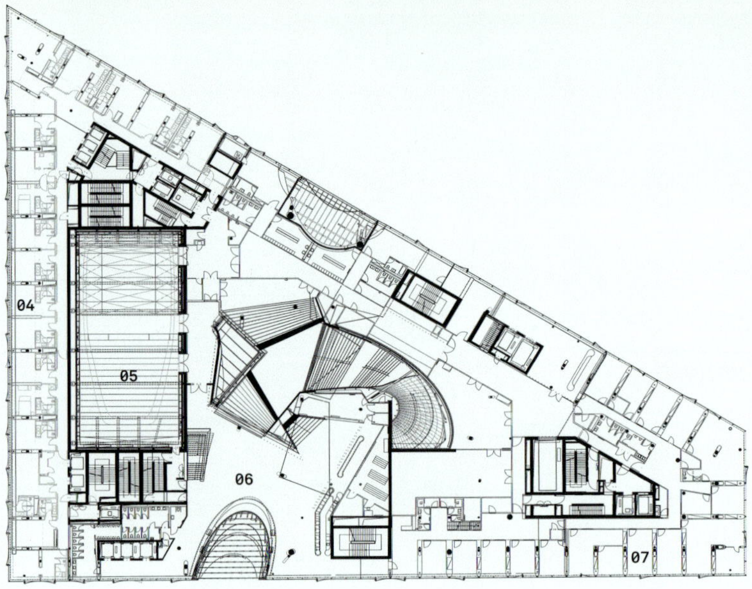

+8

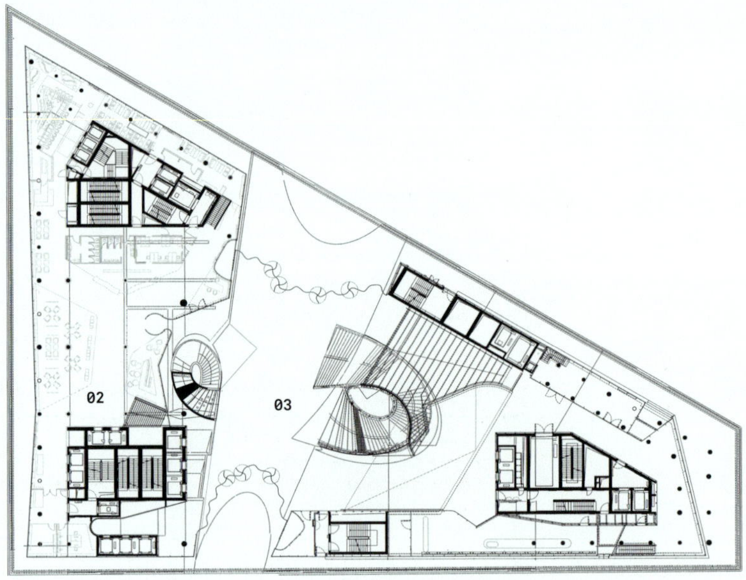

0

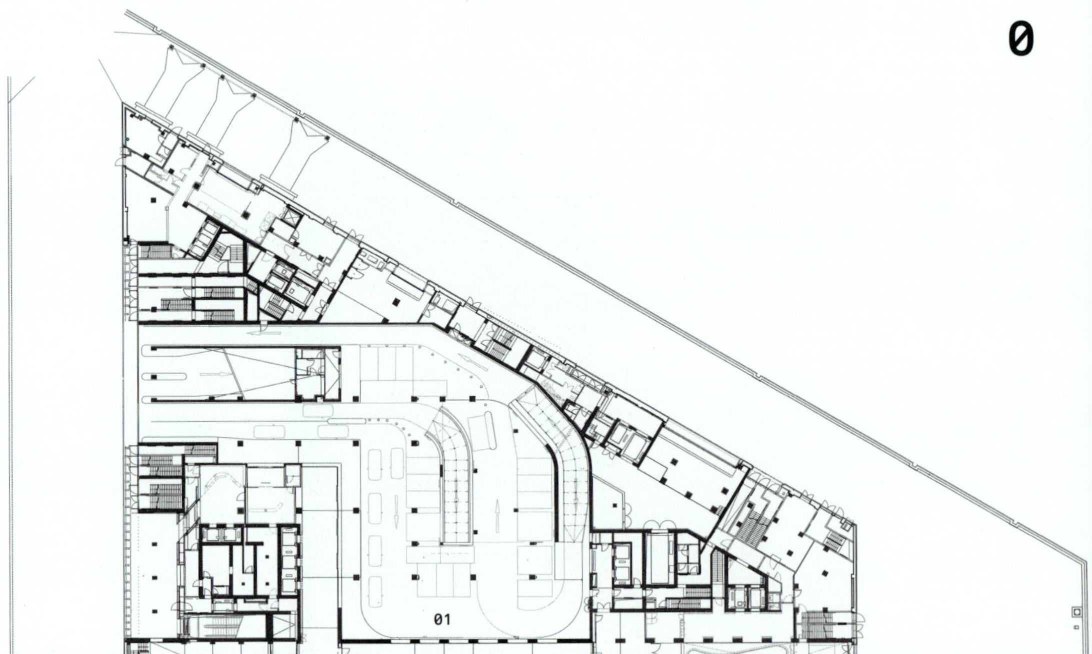

+ 16

01 Parking garage
02 Hotel foyer and bar
03 Plaza
04 Hotel rooms
05 Smaller concert hall
06 Concert hall foyer
07 Offices
08 Main concert hall
09 Apartments

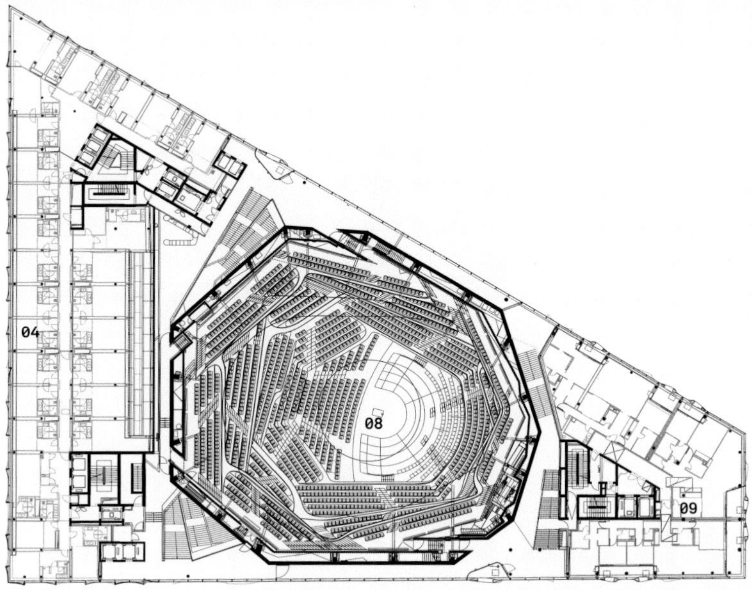

Cross Sections

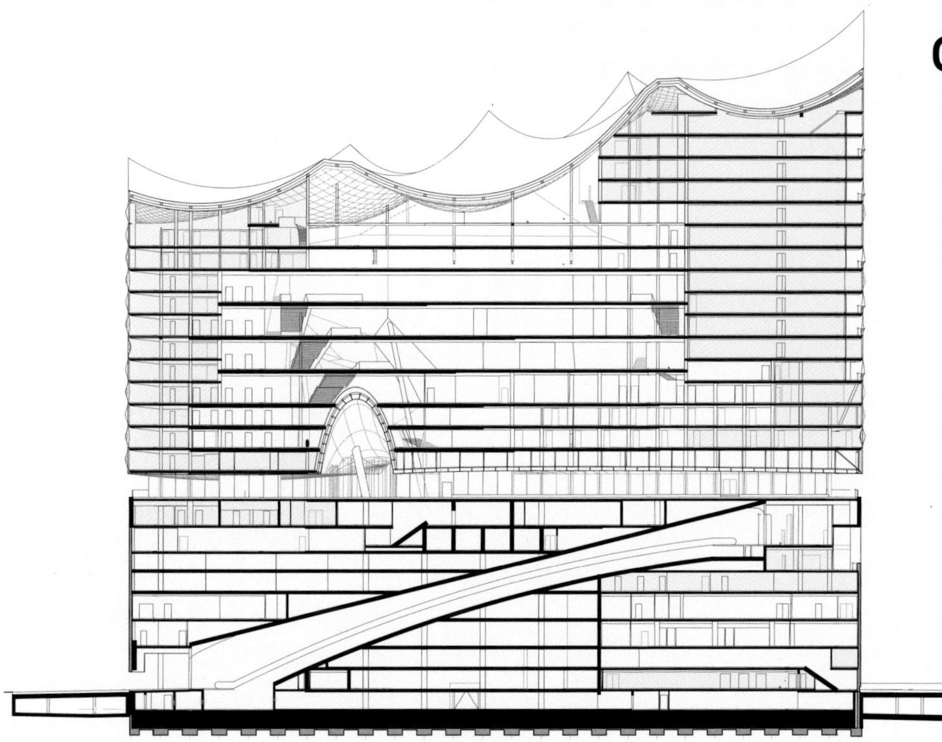

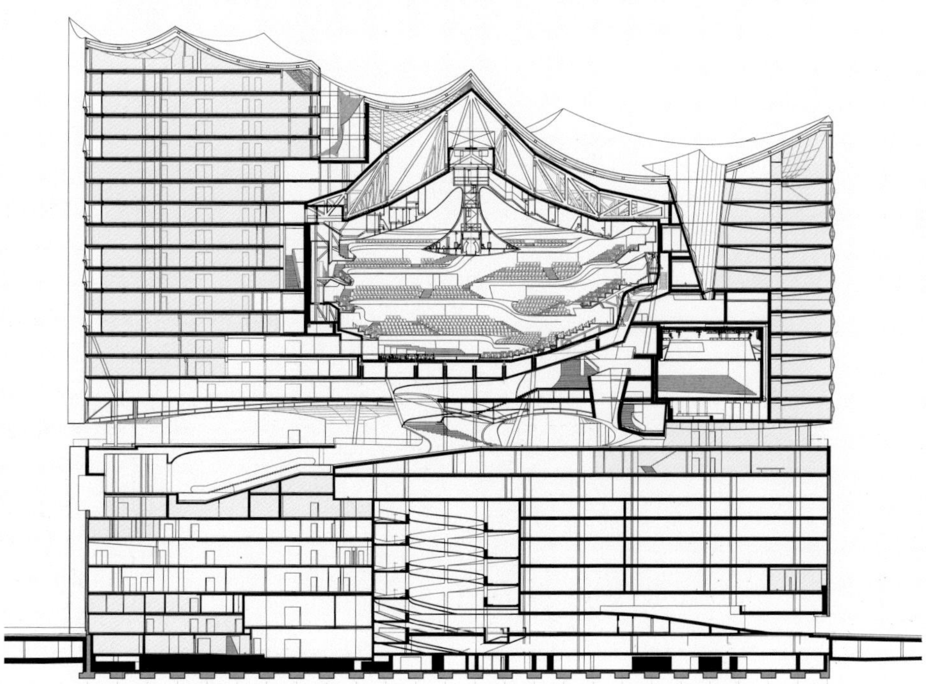

Stuttgart

Stuttgarter
fortschritt:
Verkleinerung
des jetzigen Hbf
zu einem 8 gl.
und 10.000.00
Kosten!

With Stuttgart 21, Ingenhoven turns the city's central train station from a terminal into a transit station by shifting the direction of the tracks 90 degrees and having them run underground. The project reveals errors and issues found in German planning processes.

Text
Ursula Baus

The inner city will be covered in construction dust for many more years.
Photo wilfried-dechau.de

↓ **The transformation of the station will liberate the city centre from a vast network of tracks.**
Photo Bahnprojekt Stuttgart Ulm

I

'I don't know of a single major construction project in the world that's come under as many political influences as S21,' says Manfred Leger, an industrial engineer with international experience. In the summer of 2013, Leger was hired to head S21's newly founded project association, which is responsible for completing Europe's largest infrastructure project within the next ten years: the reconstruction of Stuttgart's central train station and a new-build high-speed rail line between Stuttgart and Ulm. Of course, recent discussion concerning S21 has focused mostly (and correctly) on exploding costs, mismanagement and delays. But the historical significance of this major operation, which began in 1992, is largely political – not to mention that any infrastructure project launched over two decades ago is outdated before construction even begins.

What differentiates Stuttgart 21 from Berlin Brandenburg Airport (where noise and dirt from construction is primarily a problem of people living nearby) and from the Hamburg Elbe Philharmonic Hall (a new landmark financed in part by local residents) is that it affects the entire inner city of a German regional capital and other areas of Baden-Württemberg.

The 20th century was not good to Stuttgart, which suffered greatly from the ravages of war and from its later role as a car-friendly city. Now, nearly half the city centre is slated to be rebuilt in a mostly conventional, mono-functional way, still car-friendly, with the majority of a central park and its hundreds of old trees destroyed. Public protests that thrust such issues into the media spotlight have stemmed from many disparate factors.

↑ **The main hall of the old station, designed by Paul Bonatz, is still in use and will be preserved.**
Photo wilfried-dechau.de

↖ **Construction works started in 2010. Demolition of the station's south wing took place in April 2012.**
Photo Armin Kilgus

'The historical significance of Stuttgart 21 is largely political'

I. Original Plans

Stuttgart has been accessible by train since 1846. Only a few steps from the castle, the former seat of power, the first railway terminus was slightly more centrally situated than the existing station. It was replaced by a new building on the same site in 1868. The present terminus was erected about 500 m to the northeast during the expansion of Stuttgart from 1914 to 1928. It was designed by Paul Bonatz and Friedrich Eugen Scholer, who won an international competition with a powerful plan that was revised many times before its final realization. The quality of the Bonatz building lies in its urban plasticity; it is not a solitary structure but an integrated part of the city. The complex includes a tower, the main hall and two wings, one of which extends approximately 80 m and the other 200 m. While visiting Egypt, Bonatz had been impressed by the sleek monumentality of Egyptian construction. When the Stuttgart station was inaugurated in 1927, it attracted worldwide attention and was mentioned in the same breath as buildings by Peter Behrens and Walter Gropius. One of the largest terminus stations in Europe, with a network of 16 tracks whose construction is still impressive today, it evoked what someone called a 'mountain range of tunnels'. In 1987 the Stuttgart railway station became a listed building, and in December 2010 Gottfried Knapp, architecture critic for major German newspaper *Süddeutsche Zeitung*, called it one of the 'most important train-station constructions between historicism and modernism'.

The idea of liberating the city centre from this network of tracks has been a recurring issue. One way would be to shift the direction of the tracks 90 degrees and have them run underground, through a transit train station, but the topography of the site – which features a 'depression' – makes this plan quite complicated and expensive. In the 1980s, through tracks in the railway yard were removed, because trains were equipped with a new technology that allowed locomotives to move in both directions.

In 1990 an unexpected political constellation emerged when the CDU (conservative party) won elections in both Stuttgart and the German state of Baden-Württemberg. CDU member Heinz Dürr was the CEO of the Deutsche Bahn (German National Railways) and a native of Baden-Württemberg, as was Germany's minister of transport, Matthias Wissmann. Their collaborative decision to transform the terminus into a through station and turn it 90 degrees followed the usual procedure: feasibility study, cost prognosis, planning changes and so forth. Even then, constituents protested on grounds of high costs, technical risks, and what seemed to be disadvantageous contracts between city and railway company – far too much to discuss here. Suffice it to say that for years legal counsel has been scrutinizing every detail, whether or not justification for dispute exists.

The Project

Planning aspects of the Stuttgart 21 megaproject can be separated into three parts: the renovation of the train station, the reconstruction of the network of tracks and the redevelopment of urban areas eventually to be freed of this network.

To change the direction of the tracks and to move them underground, the station had to be redesigned and rebuilt. An architecture competition was organized in 1997, and Düsseldorf-based Ingenhoven Architects won with a plan that features a flat, subterranean system of tracks and 'lighting cones' (4.3 m high and 15 m in diameter) that allow daylight to illuminate the platforms. The 400-m-long platform hall has a ceiling height that varies from 12 to 15 m. Ingenhoven's design necessitates the demolition of the Bonatz building's two wings, both of which are important to the urban fabric of Stuttgart and which are covered by the station's listed status. Needless to say, the new plan has drawn criticism from the outset.

Underground tracks demand the construction of numerous tunnels beneath a part of town that is already densely developed. Serving a railway system that stretches from the north through the city centre (250 m above sea level) to the airport (360 m above sea level), which lies south of the Stuttgart, the project requires 57 km of new tracks, 36 km of which pass through an estimated 20 new tunnels. Some 18 new bridges are also part of the plan, as is an additional train station at the airport. →

↑ On the city square at ground level, the 'lighting cones' look like a series of sculptures.
Photos Holger Knauf

↓ The model shows flared columns, which support what the architects call 'lighting cones'. These glazed openings provide the underground platforms with natural light.

← The high speed train to Ulm and Munich goes over the Schwäbische Alb (700 m above sea level) and down the other side, reducing travel time to Ulm by about 20 minutes. Trains to Munich could stop at the airport, but that costs time. Today's travel time to Munich from Stuttgart is about two hours on well-maintained tracks; with an airport stop, only a few minutes are saved under the new plan.

Another name to consider is Herrenknecht, a Baden-Württemberg firm that is a market leader in tunnel-boring machines and a significant influence in decisions taken with regard to S21. In general, the construction lobby has been a major factor in all debates on the project.

Altogether, the project would free up about 40 hectares above ground – space that the city can develop. The Deutsche Bahn wanted to finance part of the project by selling a portion of the rail yard. Advocates of the idea see a chance for new construction and workplaces to occupy the newly available land. Urban-planning competitions for the area have yielded chiefly conventional plans that would generate more automotive traffic. At Rosensteinpark, a short distance from the heart of town, people are talking about alternative housing concepts.

Expenses have been massive, reflecting the burgeoning costs of the Elbe Philharmonic and the latest Berlin airport. The budget has risen from an initial 4.8 billion DM (€2.5 billion) to the current estimate of €10 billion. These numbers have been played down by the railway company and the government, of course, in an effort not to fuel the opposition's fire. And for two financial partners – the state of Baden-Württemberg and the city of Stuttgart – a clause for termination (on €4.5 billion of the funds) became politically explosive. In a November 2011 referendum, however, 58.9 per cent of the population voted to finance the project through the state.

Protests

The opponents of Stuttgart 21 gather every Monday for demonstrations, which escalated in 2010 when the police used inappropriate violence against the protesters. The opponents do not form a homogeneous group. Those who want to protect the park defend the trees by staging highly creative happenings. Others reject the reconstruction of the Bonatz building, even though its status as a listed building has already been tarnished by such additions as a shopping mall. One group believes the rail project is outdated in terms of mobility and technology, and another sees no sensible connection between the cost of the project and its use.

S21 has become a casus belli. Philosophically and dialectically, it expresses an old European situation in which one takes a position against change in the routine of everyday life. In Stuttgart, though, it's developed into an argument that, right or wrong, no longer does justice to modern European thinking and is going around in an endless circle of alternatives. This has been and still is the fatal flaw in the management of the project; instead of keeping an eye out for alternatives, the planners have followed a 'close your eyes and keep going' strategy – a tactic that backfired during the state parliamentary elections of 2011, which were considered a decision for or against S21. The political opponents of the project won, not only in the state parliamentary elections but also in Stuttgart's mayoral election, which saw the Green Party oust the CDU, the party that had been in power for decades. The political shift seemed to hinge on how voters felt about S21. When had a German election ever been decided by a construction project? The two sides were so calcified and polarized that in November 2010 a spectacular 'mediation' was accepted by everyone. To date, new project manager Manfred Leger appears to have recognized what's on the line in Stuttgart – a politically clear decision on how its people live and how they want to move into the future.

II. Current State of Affairs

The new state and city governments have agreed to comply with the original contracts drawn up with the official client, the Deutsche Bahn. The Deutsche Bahn emphasizes that many planning and building contracts are not subject to change, despite a budget that's run into the billions. Construction continues slowly in a huge urban operation that is bound to have all sorts of problems. Initial plans suggesting that trains would be running through a new station complete with tunnels in 2012 have given way to an estimate of 'probably 2022'. New office buildings, a library and a shopping mall rise from cleared areas bordering the site, but only a few apartment buildings have been realized. After hours, the place is like a ghost town.

III. What Now?

If the concept for Stuttgart 21 were drafted today, an entirely different planning structure would be applied. The political processes of the municipal, infrastructural and mobility-based development do not work as they did 20 years ago, when S21 was approved – right over the heads of the citizens. In a city like Stuttgart, a globally relevant topic like mobility has to be rethought in a comprehensive manner. Its transport systems need intelligently designed, economically sound networks. Partial changes in the railway system won't improve the dramatic traffic situation in an inner city now covered in construction dust – and what about changes that are sure to occur within transport and mobility in future decades? Even urban planning has to be based on completely different premises these days. ←

ingenhovenarchitects.com

0

01 Existing railway station
02 Park
03 Bridge over platforms
04 Platforms and tracks
05 Offices

↑ **Cut-out section of the underground railway station.** Photo Holger Knauf

↖ **A glazed canopy marks the entrance to the station's underground platforms.** Rendering Peter Wels

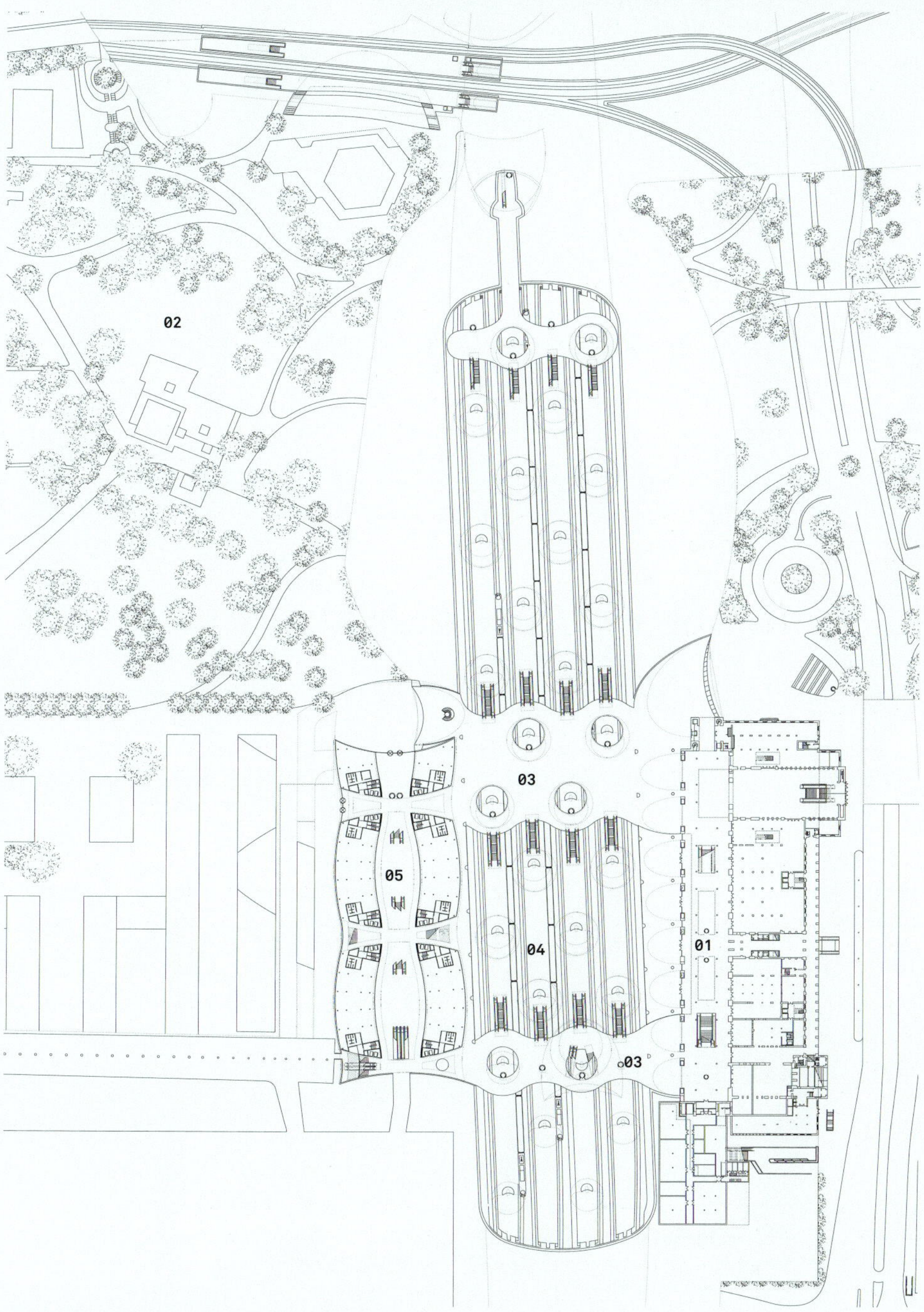

'Twenty years ago, projects were approved right over the heads of the citizens'

Site Plan

Cross Section

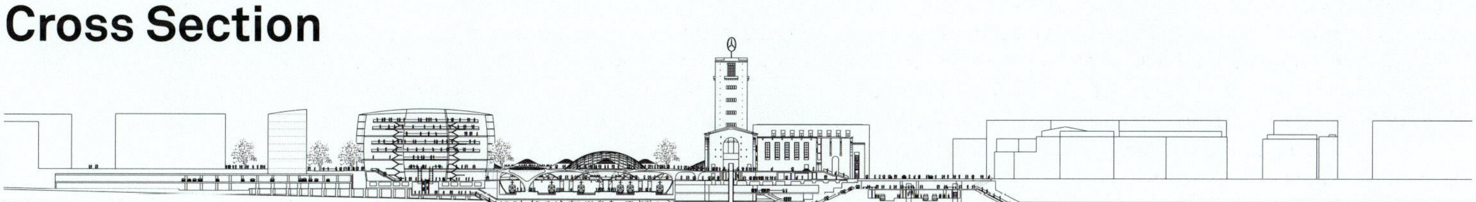

Long Section

Wiel Arets had his portrait taken by the well-known Dutch photographer Erwin Olaf.
Photo Erwin Olaf

Four new projects from Wiel Arets show the architect at the top of his cinema-inspired game.

Text
Jane Szita

'The pool moves only millimetres, even with the kids jumping up and down in it'

If we were in LA and not Marbella, somebody would surely be shooting a movie here at the Jellyfish House. In fact, it's almost as though someone already is. The scene couldn't be more perfect, or appear more choreographed. Kids are swimming overhead, in a spectacularly voyeuristic glass-bottomed pool, cantilevered out 9 m from the roof into the air towards the distant mountains. From high above, the searing Spanish sun shines through the water, throwing rippling turquoise reflections onto the terrace beneath.

The architect, Wiel Arets – wearing shorts and looking as though he's about to shout 'Cut!' – is standing in the aqueous light, beneath the surreally suspended weight of water, which he calculates at a mind-boggling 60,000 kg. 'And the pool moves only millimetres, even with the kids jumping up and down in it,' he says, clearly fascinated by the image of the blurry, distorted forms frolicking overhead. In the 38-degree heat of August in Andalusia, the house shimmers like a hallucination: the concrete is made from crushed marble and white sand. But it's not just the sun. In a region where villa architecture is on a single-mindedly twee Iberian theme, this building – overly imaginative and overtly minimal – might have landed here from outer space. 'This is the most difficult house in Spain,' says Arets, and he's surely neither exaggerating nor merely referring to the technical dimension. 'The concrete structure is tensioned for balance. The contractors were scared stiff. But then, with every project we try to push things one step further.'

Lately, a wide range of new projects by Arets' office has been landing on the pages of architecture publications and the design websites of the world. 'I'm in a publishing mood,' he says. Arets has a variety of projects in the pipeline, including a large-scale mixed-use complex near Zurich's central train station, which will be 'technically very difficult' as it will not use a single column. 'But we don't want to be this flashy office,' he stresses. A touch of Dutch anti-extravagance here, perhaps? Arets himself begs to differ: 'I don't feel like a "Dutch" architect. I feel like someone who is part of the new metropolis of the world. I live in Amsterdam, Maastricht, Zurich, Tokyo and Chicago [where he is Dean of IIT's College of Architecture]. I'm fascinated by all these places, and I can experience them only by being there.'

The 'publishing mood' extends to autobiographical and theoretical writings, in which Arets is currently as prolific as contemporary Dutch architects can sometimes be. If he writes a lot, he seems to talk even more, and much in the same style: a stream-of-consciousness sequence of ideas, observations, anecdotes and predictions. With scarcely a pause he flits from Commes des Garçons (all he's worn for the past 25 years; he was depressed for two days when a CdG shirt he'd owned for 15 years was stolen) to the future ('imagine how the flying car will change architecture – you'll suddenly have these new ways to enter a building; it will have an effect as great as the invention of the lift') to the cinematic achievements of Jean-Luc Godard (more about him later) to his own start in architecture (as a struggling two-man office, he turned down a commission for 45 houses because it was 'a terrible urban intervention', opting instead for a tiny job renovating a Maastricht store. 'I'm no businessman,' he says).

The never-ending interior monologue is how he generates ideas: 'Sitting here talking to you, in the back of my mind I'm thinking about how all this applies to our new project in Spain,' he admits. Every new project starts with Arets mulling it over 'six weeks to two months' before he's ready to even open the discussion with the project architects he appoints for every job. 'I'm someone who ideally wants to be involved in every decision.'

Like his whole oeuvre since the 1993 Maastricht Academy extension – the Tadao Ando-like work that marked his breakthrough – the latest projects aren't always easy to classify. Among the most interesting, as well as the newest of the bunch, is his biggest building so far, the Allianz Headquarters in Zurich, and there are two more modest yet intriguing and jewel-like houses in Tokyo and Maastricht, each about as different from the Jellyfish House as they are from each other.

'For me, design isn't shape, form or image; it's concept,' says Arets. 'In all our work, we start with an idea. With the Jellyfish House, we started from the idea of a reverse-order programme – the pool is on top, the guest rooms are in →

Sunshine passes through water in the swimming pool of Jellyfish House to create rippling reflections of light on the lower terrace.

↑ A ramp that begins on the street ascends to the living area. A second ramp leads down to the basement garage.

↓ The roof terrace includes permanent furniture: concrete tables, benches and day beds.

Jellyfish House

Marbella | Spain | 2013

Located in the Marbella neighbourhood of Los Monteros, on a site close to the beach but shut in by neighbouring buildings, this concrete-and-glass holiday home gains expansive views of the sea and mountains by hoisting its swimming pool to the roof, where – daringly cantilevered – it forms an extension to the terrace and a canopy for another terrace beneath.

The house is organized around three main circulation routes: the main entrance, the path from beach to roof, and the entrance for guests. Designed for indoor-outdoor living, the glazed sections of the house can be opened to allow interior and exterior spaces to flow together. This interchange, plus special green-tinted glass that blocks 90 per cent of the heat, keeps the house cool without air conditioning. The public spaces of the house, such as the living and dining rooms, and private spaces like the bedrooms, are connected by separate but intertwining circulation routes. The house provides possibilities for voyeuristic experiences in other ways as well: the glass bottom of the pool allows those on the terrace below to see the swimmers above, and the kitchen affords yet another view of the pool.

Wiel Arets is practically at home in this house; the clients are old friends. As he sees it, 'You have to feel as though you're building for yourself.' The name of the house comes from the original plan, later abandoned, which included an indoor aquarium of colourful jellyfish. In fact, humans have become the real aquarium species.

Photos Jan Bitter

'This is a time when to be an architect you have to be a bit of everything'

← the basement, because the surroundings were so built up it was the only way to get a view. The question is always, how can we make the idea work? How can we push the technical development? Not that it necessarily has to be high-tech – you don't need to see the technology.'

Pushing the technical boundaries of the Allianz Building, he relates, resulted in a new façade product – two layers of glass, with a computer-controlled layer of sunscreen curtain in between. Then there's the ceiling treatment, which has already won an innovation award. Clad in micro-perforated aluminium modular units measuring 1.35 m^2 each, it 'looks interesting, has an acoustic effect and cools the air, thanks to water pipes behind it. For this project, we had to make a lower ceiling because of the restrictions – I hate low ceilings, but if we have to do one, then let's do something new. Let's make it a challenge. And so we got a new material out of something we had to do. Technology is how we renew our thinking.'

There's a clear thematic line in Arets' work, however, not only in its generally minimalist bent but also in the architect's preoccupations with 'circulation, glass and materials', as he sums it up himself. There's tactility as well as geometry in his buildings, and what Greg Lynn calls a 'chameleon-like' quality, achieved through layering permeable zones and translucent surfaces. V' House in Maastricht, A' House in Tokyo and the Allianz Building are wrapped in different kinds of glass: textured, decorative and reflective at the same time. All three both stand out from and adopt the stamp of their surroundings. A' House's sliding doors can open its interior to the world, surrendering to what Arets calls the Japanese condition of 'seeing yet not seeing'; V' House has an open ground floor where you can drive your car and where rain is also allowed to fall. Jellyfish House has water as well as glass as part of its membrane – in this sense, perhaps it really does earn its name: jellyfish are 95 per cent water, after all.

Then there are the spatial narratives that have preoccupied Arets throughout his career. Circulation plays a major role in all his buildings, from the single entrance and routing he employed in the Maastricht Academy extension (as a means of making students and professors interact) to the complex network of paths hardwired into the design of the Allianz Building, with its bridges and stairways. Here in Jellyfish House, with a trio of staircases and volumes that repeatedly open to the outdoors, the routes can seem puzzling, labyrinthine and even Escher-like. The first path leads from the main entrance, the second is a separate entrance for guests, and a third connects the beach directly to the roof, with its pool, terrace and long concrete table that morphs into a bed. The routes link private spaces – bedrooms, bathrooms – or public ones – kitchen, lounge, the outdoors – but intertwine with one other, offering sudden unexpected snapshots of other spaces and other house inhabitants.

'It's like a movie,' says Arets as he gleefully shows off some of his favourite angles, and indeed it is. His architecture tends to frame beautifully those who use it, while offering an ever-changing sequence of experiences, some quick, some slow and some cutting unexpectedly to others, in a way suggesting the work of the director he most admires, Jean-Luc Godard. It seems he once took 300 still photos of Godard's 1960s film, *Pierrot le Fou*, saying they let him see things he didn't see in the movie. Jellyfish House is like a house of stills, its sometimes bewildering navigation drawing the attention to moments and angles that its architect will not allow to be missed. 'I think it's interesting to use different staircases for different functions,' he says. 'I always like to have three or four different routes.'

Film and photography are present in Arets' work, too, in its monochrome palette, exaggerated perspectives, graphic detailing – even in his grainy drawings and sometimes grainy surfaces, a good example being the famously black, screen-printed, glass-and-concrete façade of the Utrecht University Library. The grainy quality recurs, but then smoothed and polished, in the Allianz headquarters façade. This way or that way, open or closed, translucent or opaque: the coexistence of alternatives is perhaps the strength of Arets' work, as indeed it is of his writing and his conversation. He is clearly loathe to come to a conclusion on any topic, preferring – it seems during our conversation – to backtrack and pursue another angle. It's hard not to see the connection between the constantly talking, idea-modulating architect who appears in person and in print, and the interest in circulation. For Arets, architecture might ultimately be the challenge of breathing fluidity into monumentality; his buildings reveal themselves only as you move through them. Jellyfish House lives in the memory as a beguilingly liquid experience – and not just because of the pool on the roof.

Liquid – or at least in a state of flux – is how Arets ultimately regards his position as an architect, at any rate. 'People regard architecture as an autonomous discipline,' he says, 'but I think we can learn a lot from materials science or medicine. I myself studied physics before I decided to become an architect. Why do we no longer ask which philosophers are interesting? It's because we can no longer talk of "the philosopher". It's the same with architecture; we can't isolate the discipline any more. This is a time when to be an architect you have to be a bit of everything.' ←

wielaretsarchitects.com

‘Design isn’t shape, form or image; it’s concept’

↑ Among the many stairways in this house is a scissor stairs.

↖ The living room is right next to the entrance.

→ Sightlines connect the kitchen with the living room and the swimming pool overhead.

'This is the most difficult house in Spain'

Cross Sections

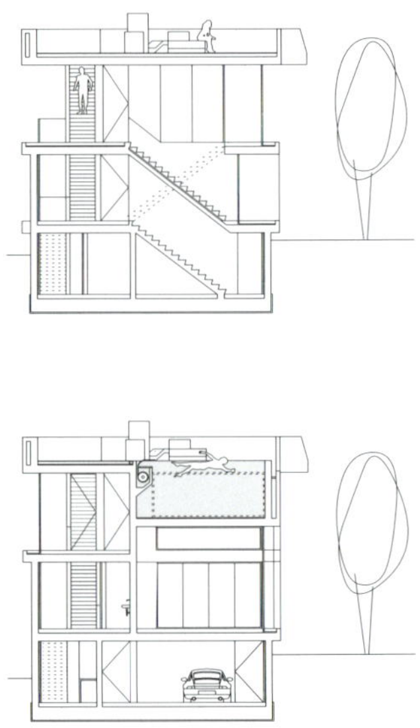

Long Section

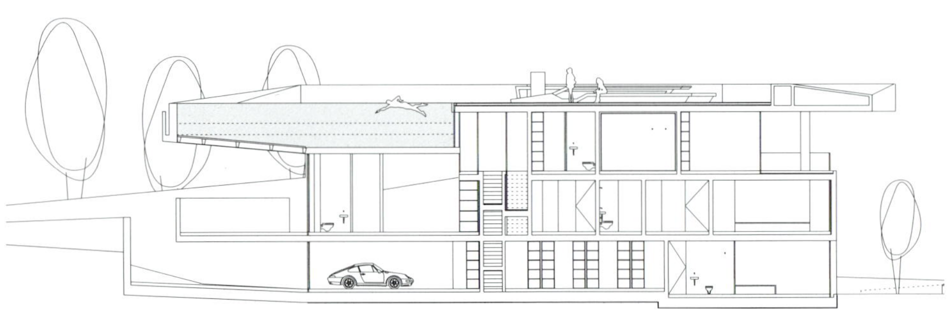

+2

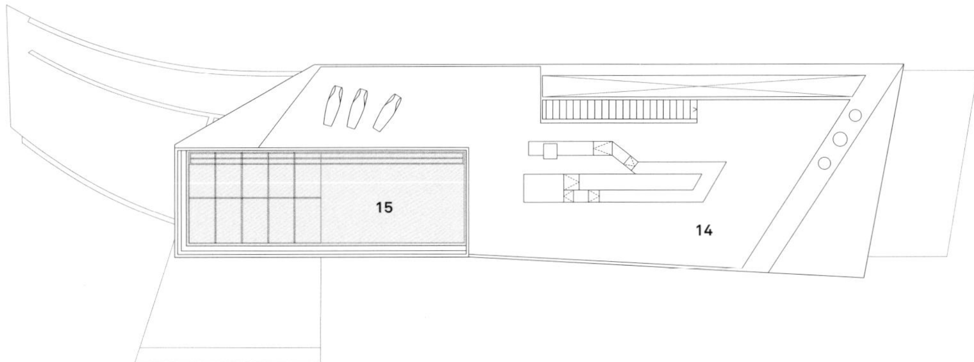

+1

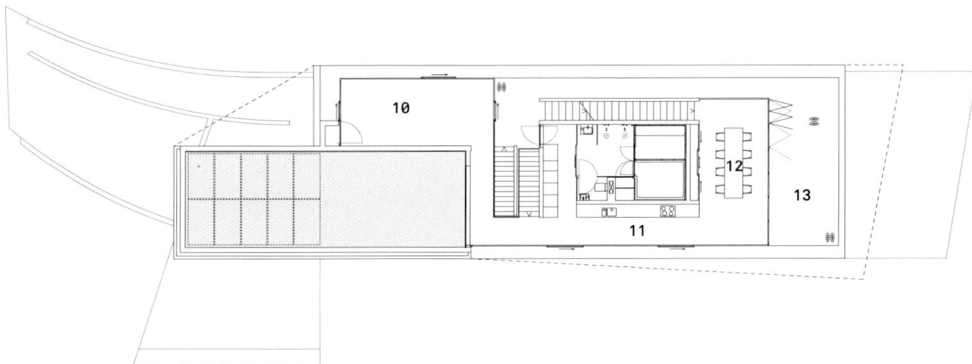

0

01 Garage
02 Storage
03 Guest bedroom
04 Terrace
05 Entrance hall
06 Living room
07 Children's bedroom
08 Master bedroom
09 Bathroom
10 Office
11 Kitchen
12 Dining room
13 Patio
14 Roof terrace
15 Swimming pool

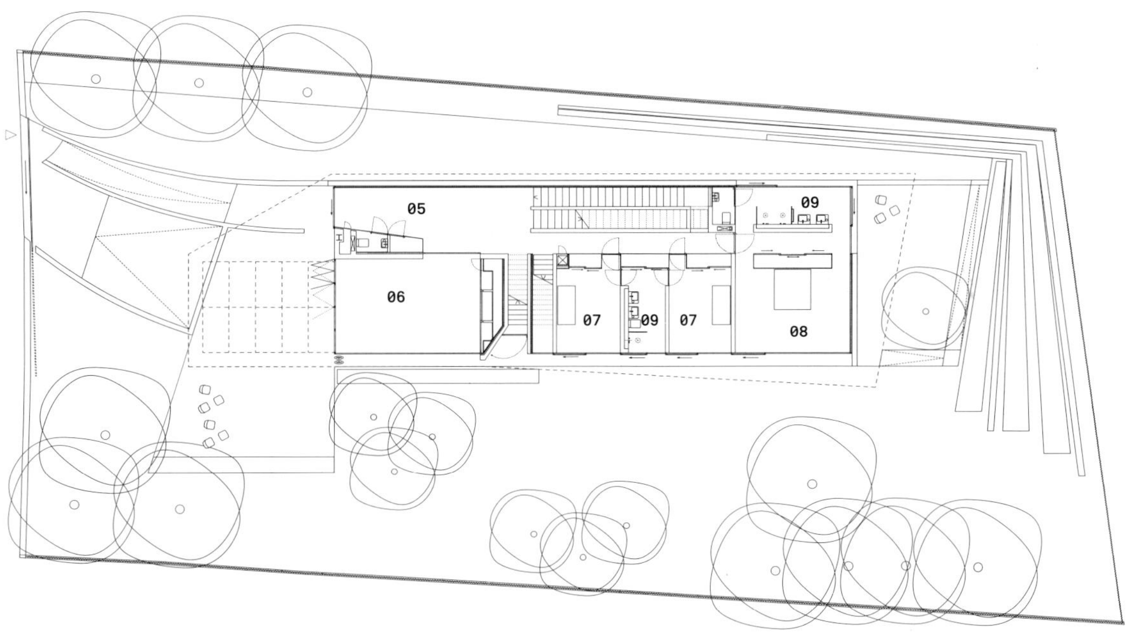

−1

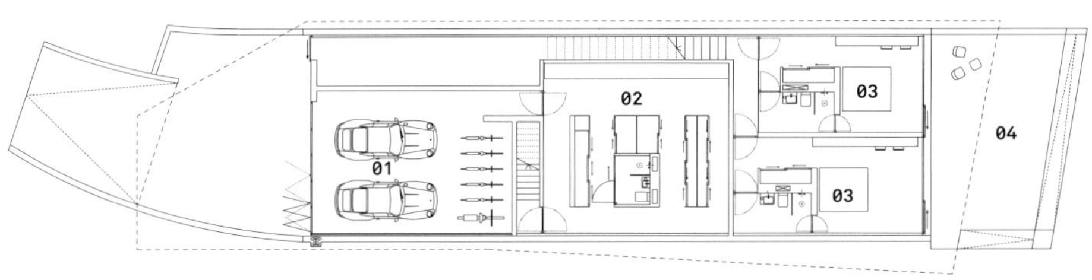

V' House
Maastricht | Netherlands | 2013

Located in the heart of Maastricht, where building regulations dictate that new projects must correspond to the existing context, V' House began its life as a warehouse. Arets created voids that permit natural light to enter the building and improve air circulation. A large cutout in the main façade forms a triangular surface that leads from the sloped roof of V' House to the vertical wall of the adjacent property. Surrounded by brick buildings, the house is a glass insertion into the historical urban fabric.

Designed for clients who collect vintage automobiles, V' House has an entrance that doubles as a covered carport large enough for several vehicles. Access to the house is provided by a shallow staircase to the first floor. A secondary circulation route consisting of a lift and a staircase allows for vertical short cuts. Sliding doors measuring 3 x 3 m perforate the façade, complemented by highly polished concrete.

Photos Jan Bitter

↑ The storey containing the living area hangs from two large steel beams that span the entire width of the property. These two steel members rest on columns in the garden wall.

← V' House has a screen-printed glazed façade that resembles curtains.

↗ The living area occupies one uninterrupted space.

+2

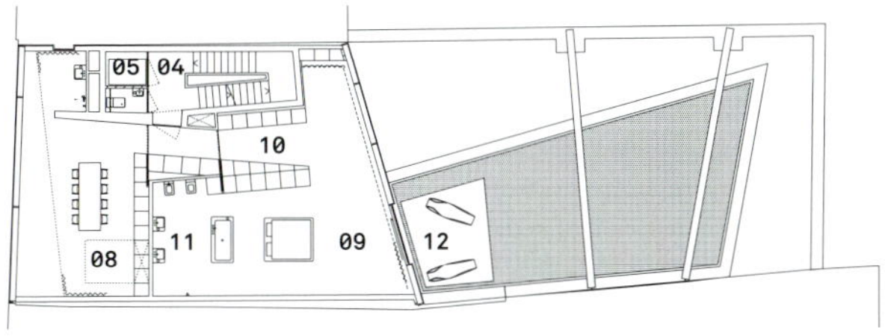

+1

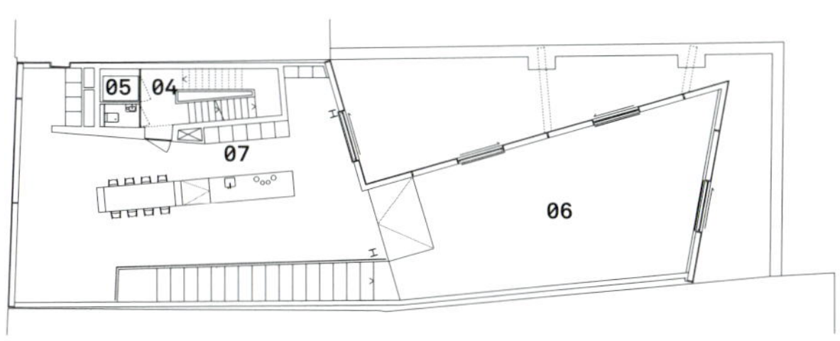

0

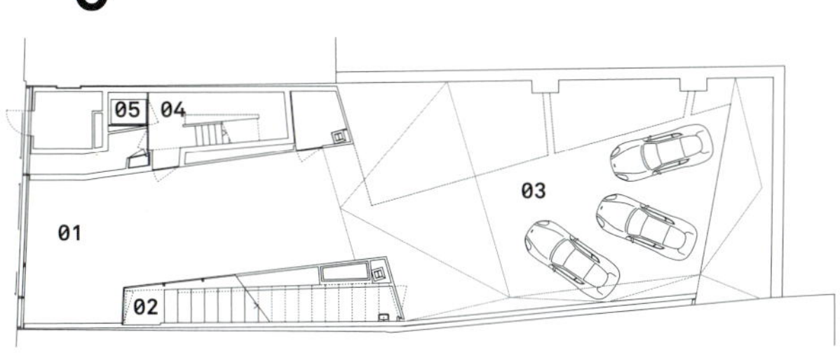

01 Entrance hall
02 Main entry stairs
03 Garage
04 Stairwell
05 Lift
06 Living room
07 Kitchen
08 Office
09 Bedroom
10 Closet
11 Bathroom
12 Roof terrace

Long Section

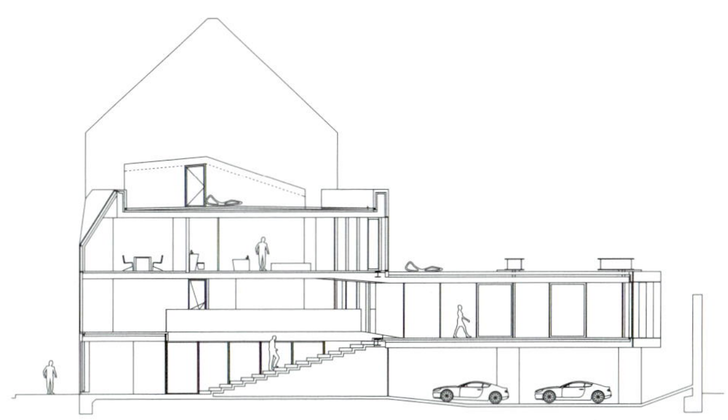

+3

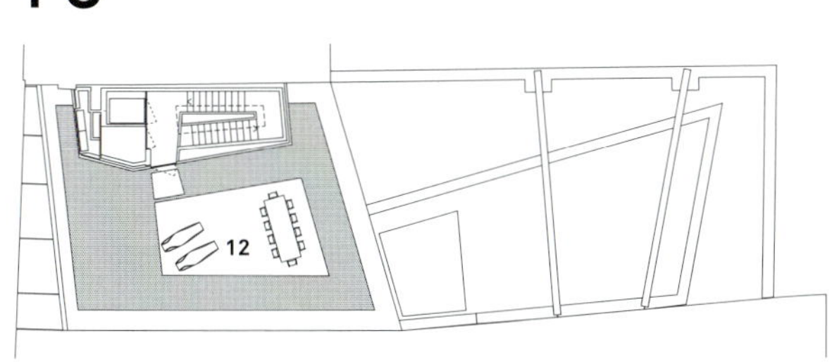

Allianz Headquarters

Wallisellen | Switzerland | 2013

The hybrid programme occupies two buildings, a high-rise and a six-storey structure, which are linked by a series of bridges that enable the various offices, employee amenities, retail facilities, restaurants and cafés to be easily accessed and fluidly interrelated.

Beginning in the main entrance hall, which accommodates a large staircase that rises 72 m through the building, the horizontal layering of office floors opens up and spaces are connected through a series of vertical voids that link the separate floors visually and physically. These multistorey voids create short cuts between floors through the use of open stairways, which produce varied spatial relations and connections throughout the building.

Circulation to and from these stairs and voids is towards and perpendicular to the outer glass skin, while circulation on each floor takes place along and parallel to the façade, so that both buildings are constantly alive with movement. The exterior silk-screened glazing comprises two layers, which sandwich a computer-controlled, sun-screening curtain.

Photos Jan Bitter

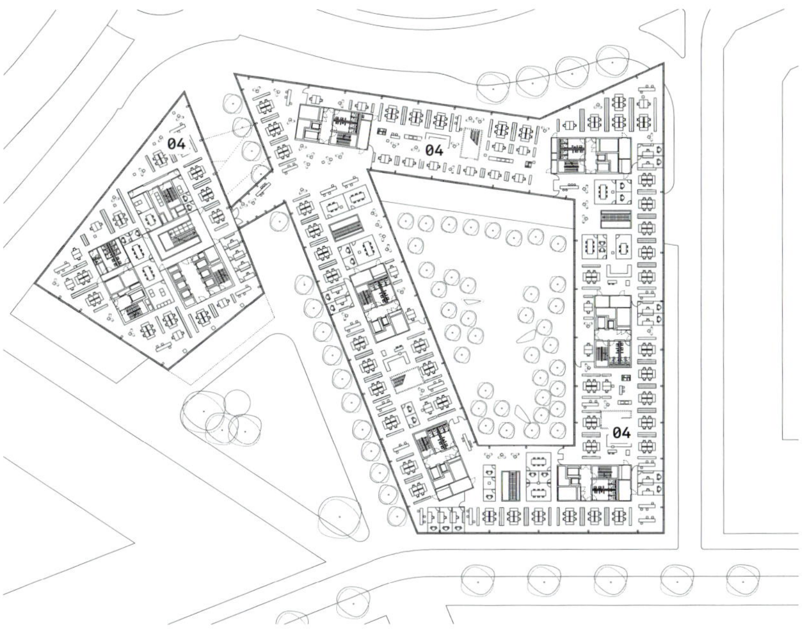

+2

Long Section

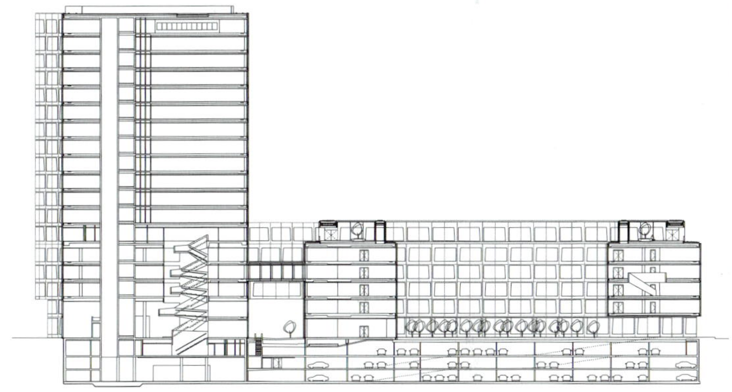

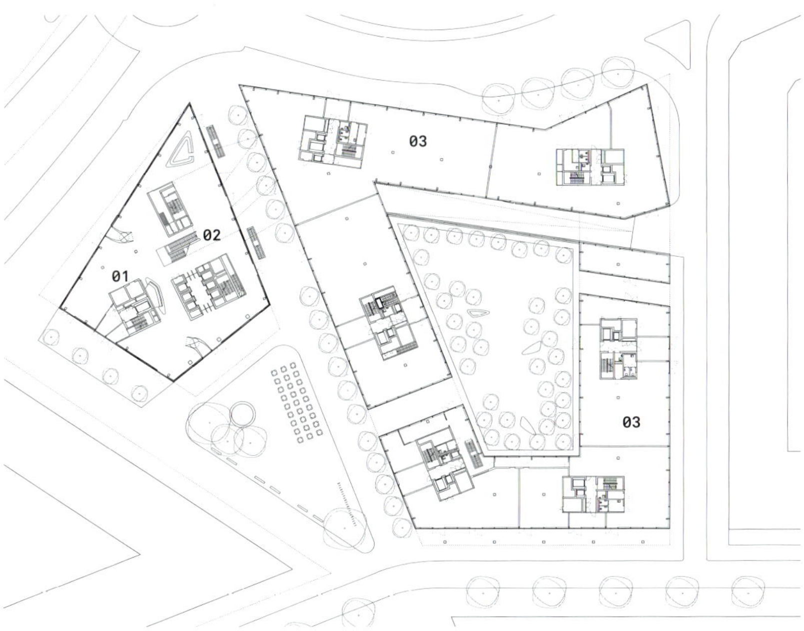

0

01 Main entrance hall
02 Main staircase
03 Commercial space
04 Offices

↑ The headquarters of global insurance company Allianz are on Neue Winterthurerstrasse in Wallisellen, a suburb of Zurich.

← Footbridges at the Allianz complex connect the six-storey volume with the high-rise building.

↑ Large sliding doors made from relief glass function as shutters, which can be used to close off the world outside. The windows behind these shutter-doors are made from ordinary plate glass.

→ The living room on the first floor, with the shutter-doors closed.

A' House

Tokyo | Japan | 2013

A' House, which Arets designed for his family and himself, occupies a corner lot in Nishi-Azabu, a high-density, rapidly gentrifying neighbourhood in central Tokyo. With south- and west-facing façades, the house is in an area characterized by low-rise residential housing and narrow streets, close to a large park. The concrete structure is wrapped in relief glass whose white-printed, purpose-designed pattern gives the house its monolithic appearance. The south end of the residence features an outdoor terrace, which is also within the white envelope that encloses the rest of A' House.

Photos Bas Princen

Cross Section

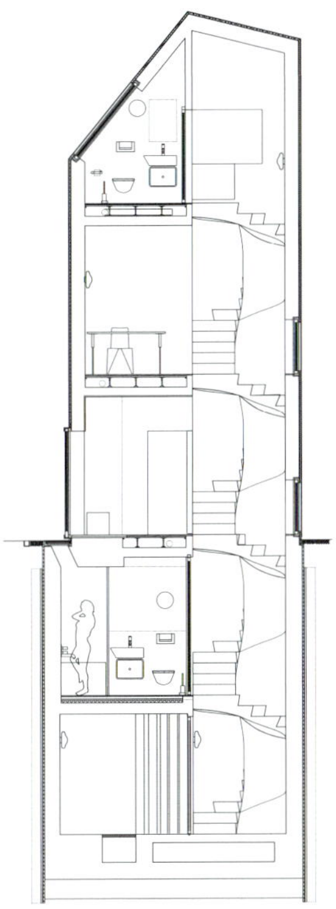

Long Section

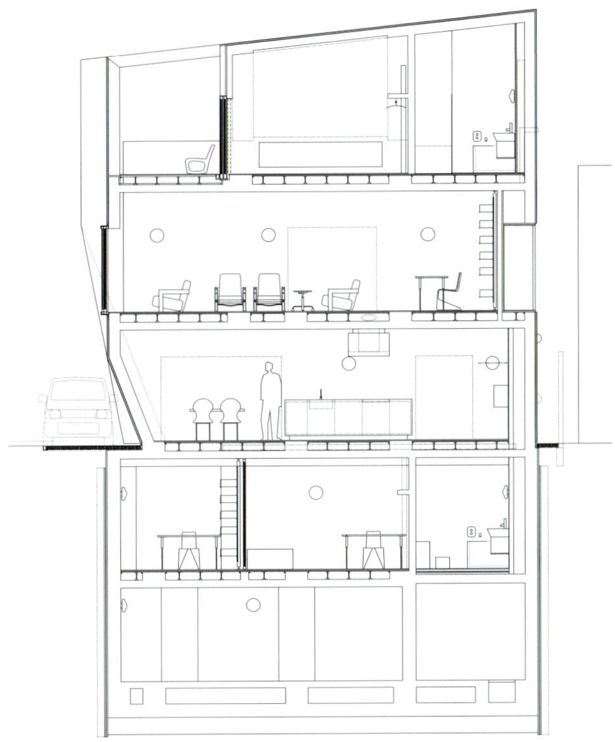

+2

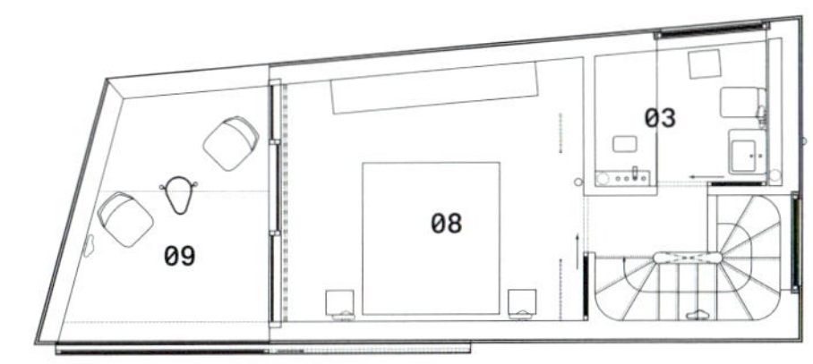

+1

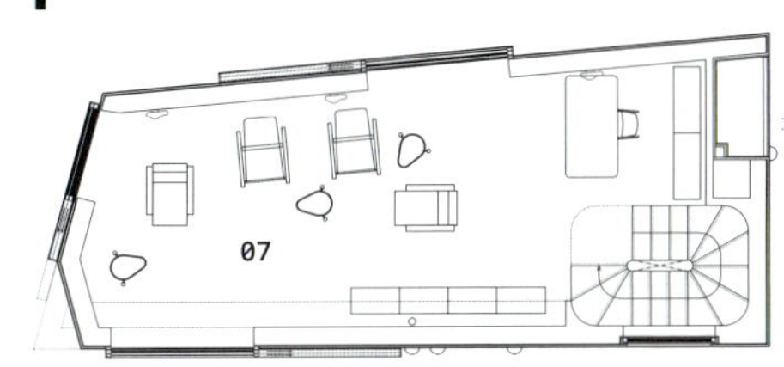

0

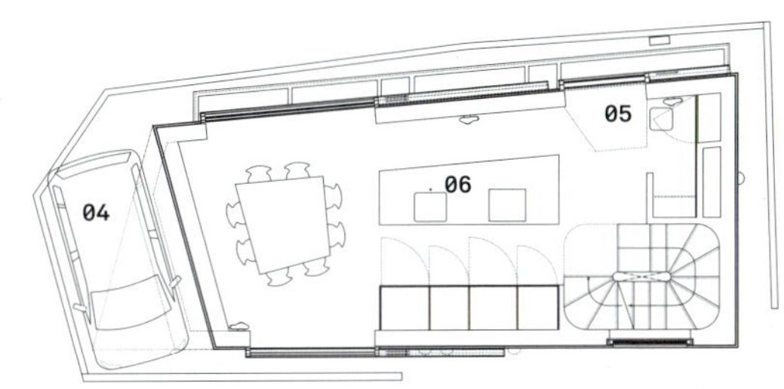

−1

01 Storage
02 Children's bedroom
03 Bathroom
04 Parking
05 Entrance
06 Kitchen
07 Living room
08 Master bedroom
09 Terrace

−2

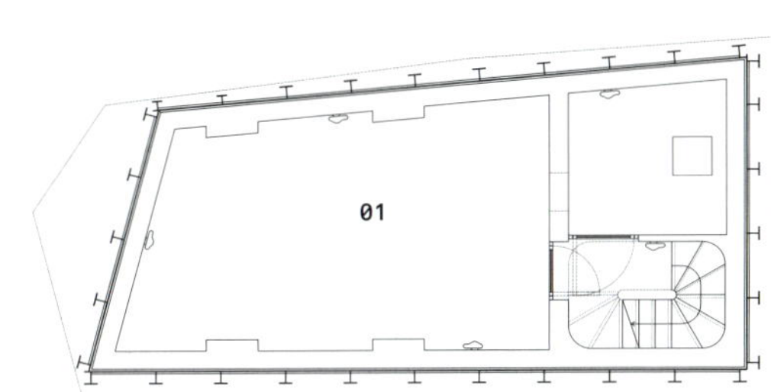

Longing for a Landmark

The commission for a massive museum in the Chinese city of Taiyuan permitted Preston Scott Cohen to go wild.

Text and Photos
Sergio Pirrone

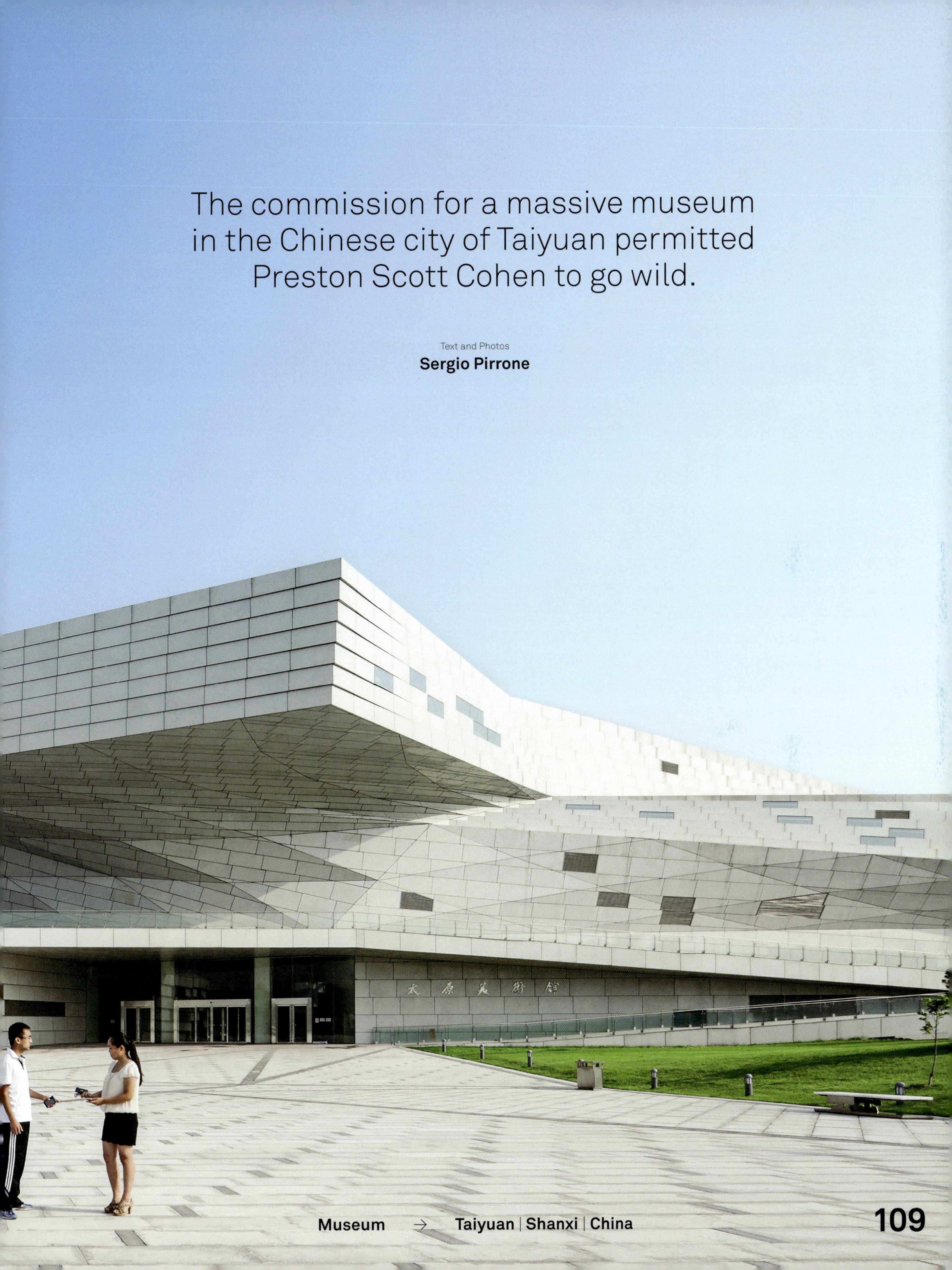

↑ The museum is next to the Fen, a broad river that transects the city of Taiyuan.

O

On my way to Taiyuan, the capital of Shanxi Province in Northern China, I'm wondering what to expect. Every time I venture into inner China, I have mixed feelings – a sense of excitement tempered by the apprehension that often rises when facing the unknown.

At night, Taiyuan is a black canvas against which a rainbow of neon ideograms spills its light. Situated on the Fen River and boasting over four million inhabitants, Taiyuan currently has a GDP with an average annual growth rate of 8 per cent, representing a momentum great enough to reshape the city substantially. At its centre lies Fen River Park, a green mixed-used waterfront area about 500 m wide and 6 km long. Lengthwise, it stretches from Shengli Bridge in the north to Changfeng Bridge in the south, where it meets the main artery of the Changfeng District, which holds the future of Taiyuan. As the central business district, Changfeng is the city's answer to Chaoyang in Beijing or Lujiazui in Shanghai.

Tackling the idiosyncratic chaos of urban China, planners in Taiyuan are addressing what Richard Ingersoll calls

‘Sprawltown’, along with the need for attractive, centralized cultural programmes with a potential for the development of iconic architecture, striking landmarks and city symbols. Among these buildings is the new Taiyuan Museum of Art designed by Preston Scott Cohen.

Only a few minutes’ walk from the DNA-shaped Zhonghuan Bridge, the 52-year-old Boston-based architect’s latest project is ‘a cluster of buildings unified by continuous and discontinuous promenades both inside and outside’. When I speak to Cohen, he recalls the moment in 2007 when everything began. While visiting Steven Holl’s Beijing branch, Li Hu, who headed the office at that time, asked Cohen to consider replacing Holl’s team in a competition for the Taiyuan Museum of Art, which the team had neither the time nor the inspiration to enter. Two days later, while lecturing at Southeast University in Nanjing, Cohen received a call from the competition organizer, officially inviting him to replace Holl.

The municipal authorities of Taiyuan had chosen an open area as the future site of five cultural buildings. Although the piece of land was no more than a muddy field, it had been the subject of an earlier master plan that referred to it as the ‘Green Cultural Island’. The design of each of the five buildings was to follow a distinctive language of form, different from that of the other four.

Unlike other North American architects, such as Holl and Thom Mayne, Cohen had no track record in China and was an absolute outsider. ‘The competition schedule was ridiculously short. We made a mad rush to visit Taiyuan a couple of times in order to meet the competition requirements, and our submission of the final design was the poorest presentation of any we’ve done since. So, why did we win? I have asked myself and others many times – without receiving a convincing answer.’

As a separate competition was organized for each of the five buildings and the vast area involved offered the architects no specific reference points, the ‘distinctive languages of form’ had to be developed without comprehensive guidance. Rather than attempting to establish an explicit relationship →

↑ Preston Scott Cohen made the Taiyuan Museum of Art part of the Fen River Park. A large opening on one side of the building lends access to the sculpture garden.

↗ Façades are clad in lightweight honeycomb panels with a laminated stone veneer.

← with any of the other four buildings, Cohen envisioned the museum as part of a parklike landscape and, more specifically, as a 'threshold' within Fen River Park. He speaks of the project as 'a thick, horizontal, topographic form' – a 'knot that defines a path through, rather than into, the building'.

Because competition restrictions pertained only to setbacks and heights, the architect spread out the building, keeping it as close to the ground as possible, and used gently inclined ramps to reinforce its low-lying silhouette. With the exception of a peak at the centre of the building, the museum is conspicuously lower than its neighbours. From afar, it seems to sink, generating an 'absent space', particularly in comparison with the other four cultural venues. Close up, it appears to undergo internal tensions that lift it from or press it to the earth. 'In 2007, during my first trip to Taiyuan, I met Luo Ke, a student who kindly offered to accompany me from Nanjing and to help me communicate effectively,' says Cohen. 'He also introduced me to the agricultural history of Shanxi Province, which inspired our design of the museum.'

The shape of the building is generated by a spline that makes a quatrefoil whose gaps are filled by hyperbolic parabolas. The spline itself is extruded vertically, creating twisted surfaces. Cohen clad the main areas in diamond-shaped panels and the hypars in folded panels.

'A combination of different types of cladding was new to me at the time,' says Cohen, 'nor had I seen the effect produced by lightweight honeycomb panels with a laminated stone veneer.' Because of their size, the 2-m-long panels give the impression of a building with 'a very unusual scale'. The panels look too large to be made of stone and too flat to be made of metal. The multifaceted exterior surfaces are pushed out by internal pressures and held back by a complex steel frame that includes skewed and stacked Vierendeel trusses.

Nothing merges and nothing remains constant in the design of the Taiyuan Museum of Art, although all relationships are interdependent. Cohen's hyperkinetic volumes react to an immobile ground and suffer dramatic and disarticulated struggles, as if they were arms pulling and tugging at other

'My architectural investigations demand building on a large scale'

arms, with a skin stretched by such efforts. Cohen speaks of a repetitive exercise of 'compression-decompression-expansion, where the spatial oscillation between high and low has been used to articulate the sequence of the building'. In his opinion, the museum's spaces 'are constricted far more than what is normally found in large public buildings in China'.

After passing beneath a towering cantilevering canopy, which contains the restaurant, you walk through an exceedingly low entrance, enveloped within a sense of intimacy. The ceiling inside soars upward but descends to a very low level before you reach the final vertical upsweep that marks the monumental atrium. The entire complex revolves around this atrium and the museum's large inner courtyard.

In describing the exterior promenade, the American architect mentions Le Corbusier's Carpenter Center in Cambridge, Massachusetts, and James Stirling's Neue Staatsgalerie in Stuttgart. Here in Taiyuan, the outdoor promenade allows people to bypass the museum on their walk through the green surroundings. An interior promenade, however, invites us to ascend a set of ramps that begin on the ground floor of the atrium, and to visit the galleries along the way. Visitors can experience the museum as a continuous sequence or choose to skip one or more clusters of galleries.

In more philosophical terms, Cohen talks about 'visual revelation and concealment versus physical access and temporarily denied physical access' and says that 'the dialectic between continuity and discontinuity is the key to the experience of the building'. In any case, this was his answer to the municipal demand for an 'oversized' museum. He realizes that the Taiyuan project has given him the opportunity to build 'on a large scale that corresponds to my architectural investigations'. The complex 3D configurations and elaborate ramped promenades that are features of his work, he says, need large buildings to manifest themselves in a convincing way. ←

pscohen.com

The museum forms a proscenium-cum-passageway for and through the surrounding park. In the background (left) is the theatre that Arte Charpentier completed last year.

‘The dialectic between continuity and discontinuity is the key to the experience of the building’

↑ Visitors can choose to follow the interior promenade without entering the galleries.

← View of the atrium from the foyer.

→ The museum’s main function is to exhibit the work of contemporary artists from Shanxi Province, but it also shows the work of artists from other parts of China and hosts exhibitions that feature international names.

+ 2

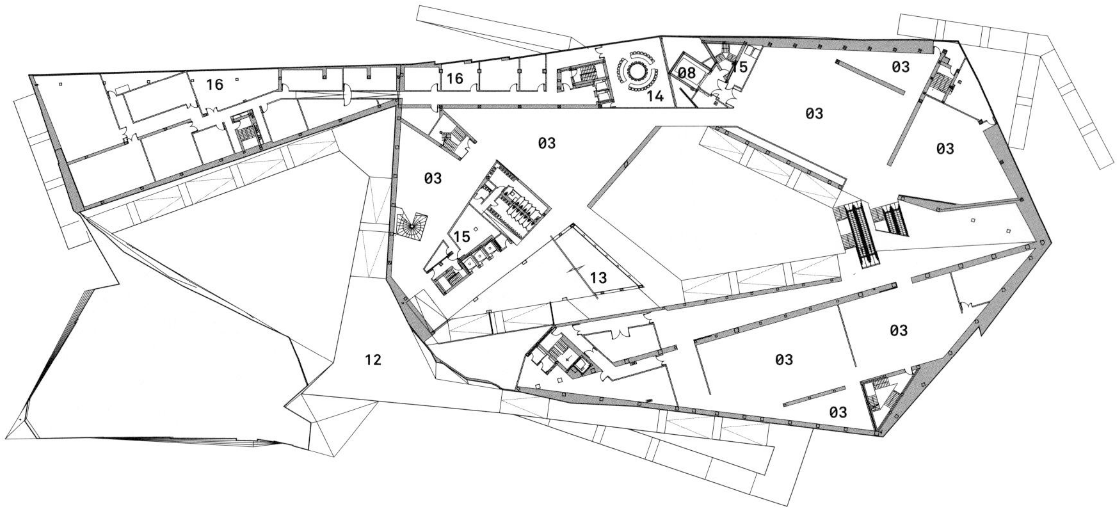

+ 1

0

01 Entrance
02 Atrium
03 Gallery
04 Shop
05 Sculpture garden
06 Auditorium
07 Foyer
08 Freight lift
09 Tunnel to galleries on the other side of the sculpture garden
10 Escalator to basement
11 Library
12 Passageway with viewing terrace
13 Roof garden
14 Conference room
15 Mechanical systems
16 Education centre
17 Administration
18 Kitchen
19 Restaurant
20 Patio
21 Stairs to roof terrace

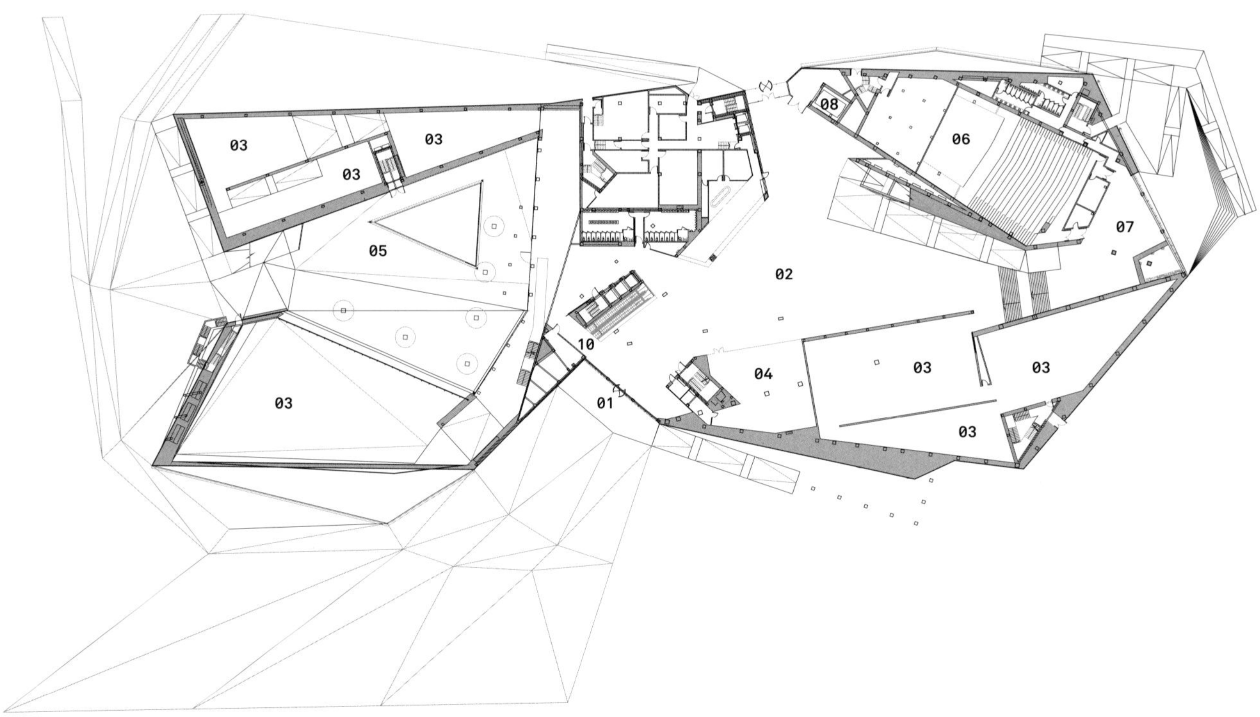

+ 4

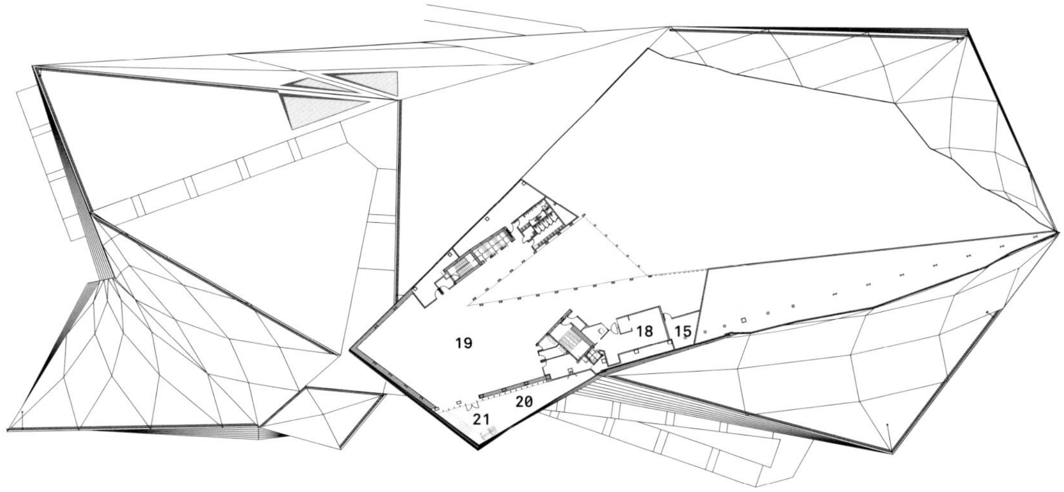

+ 3

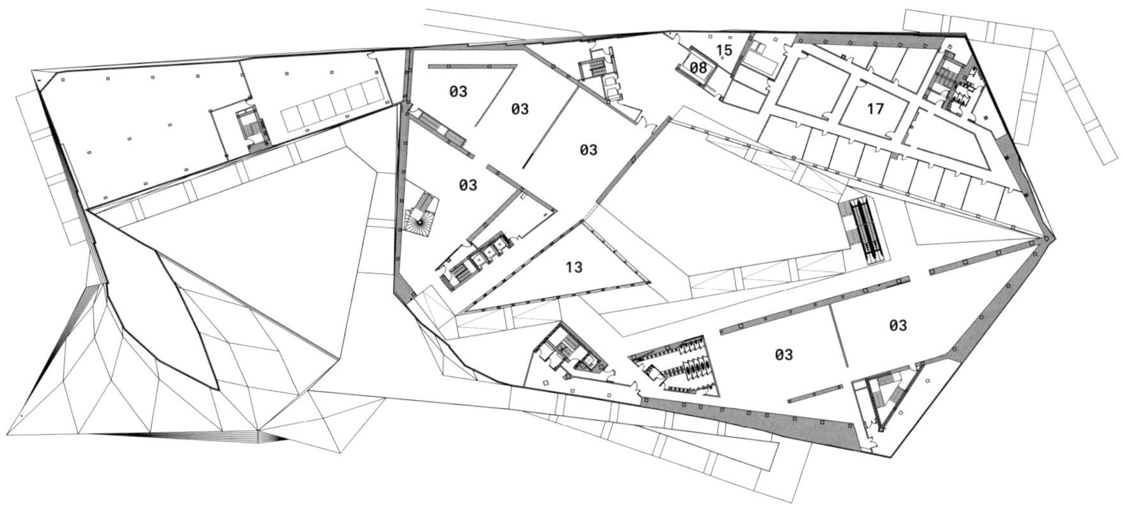

Site

Preston Scott Cohen's museum is one of five large buildings located in Taiyuan's 'Green Cultural Island'; others include a theatre by Arte Charpentier Architectes and an archaeological museum by Paul Andreu.

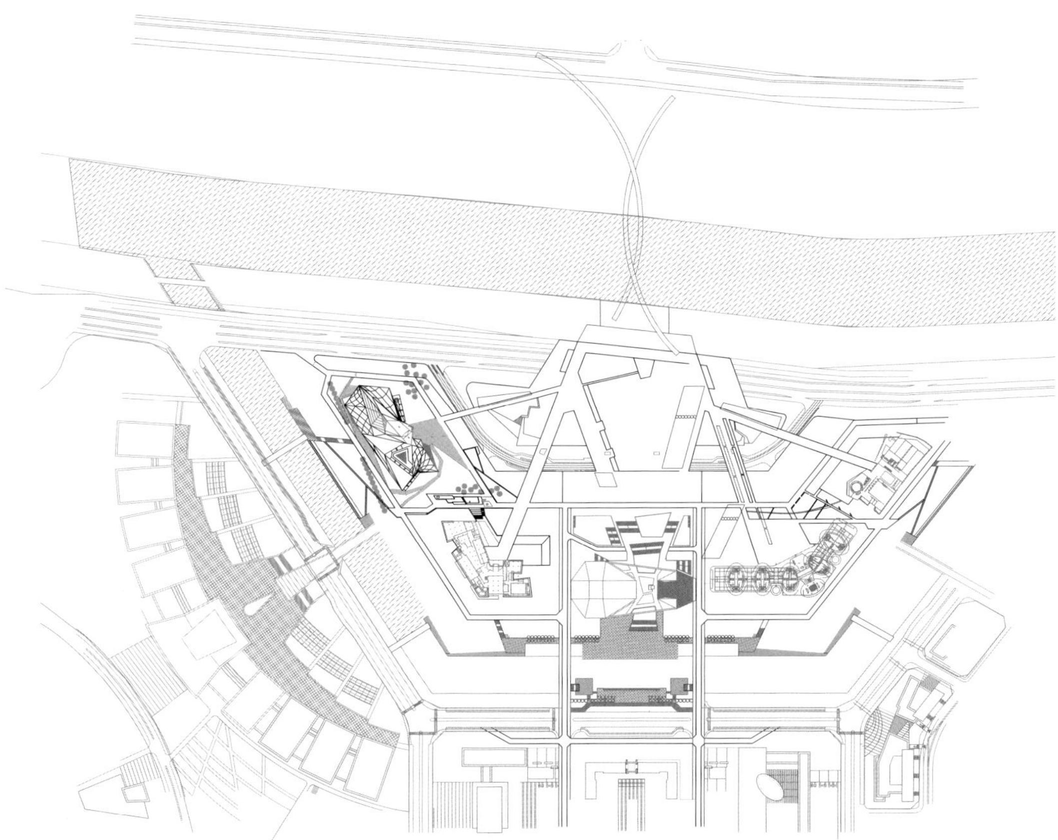

Cross Sections

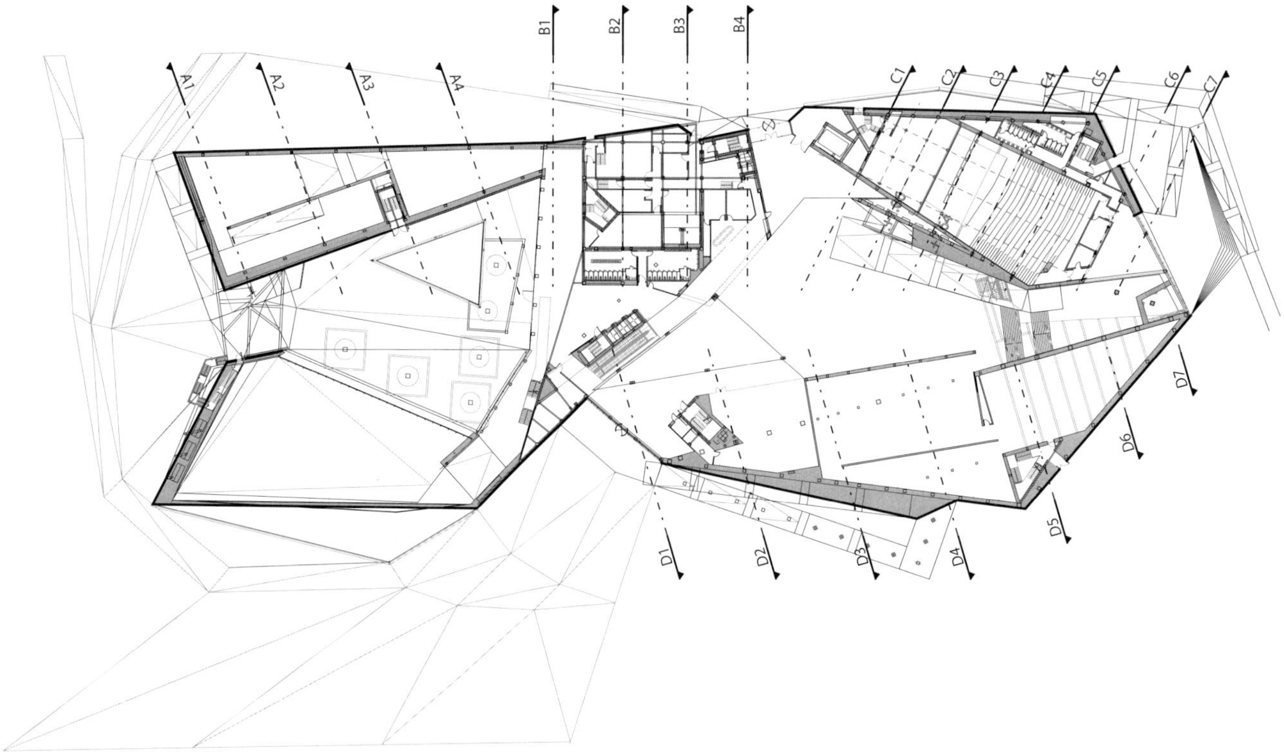

A1

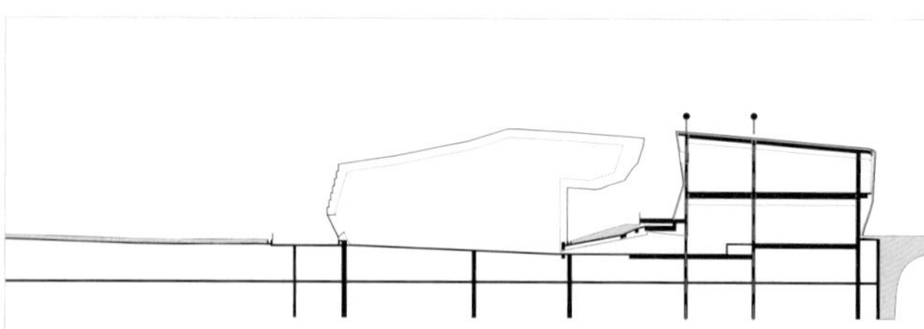

B1

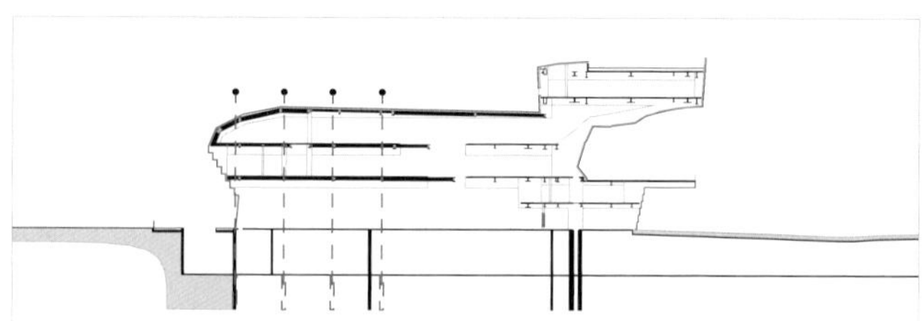

A2

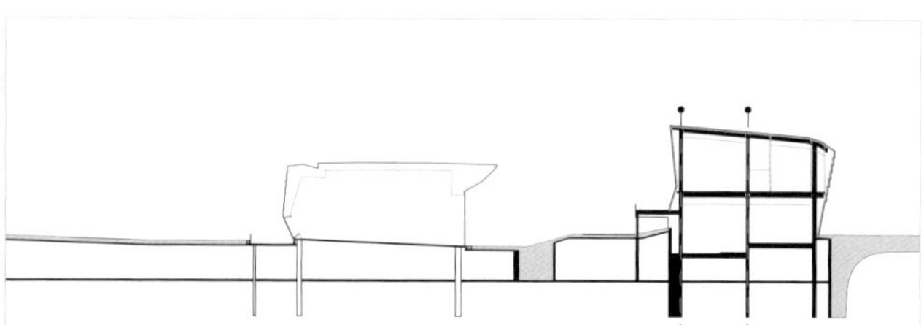

B2

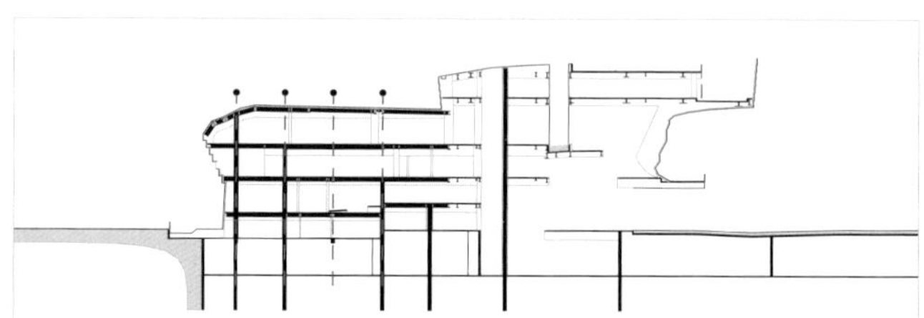

A3

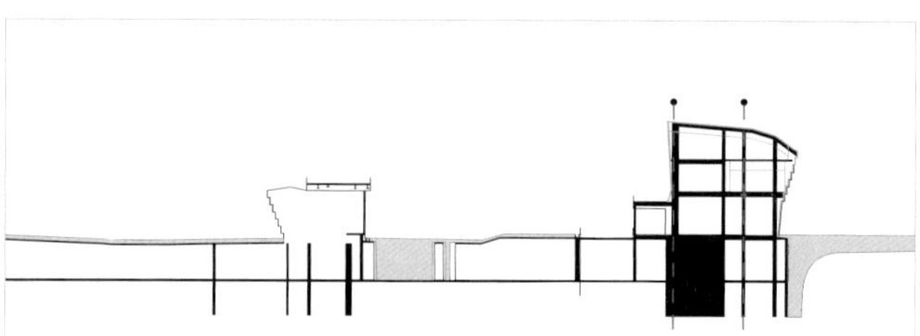

B3

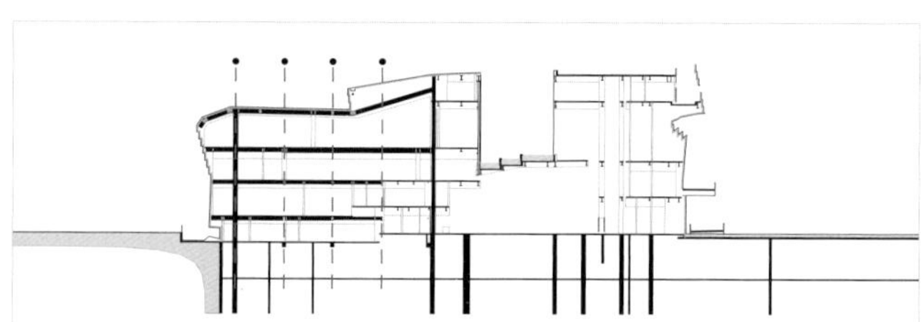

A4

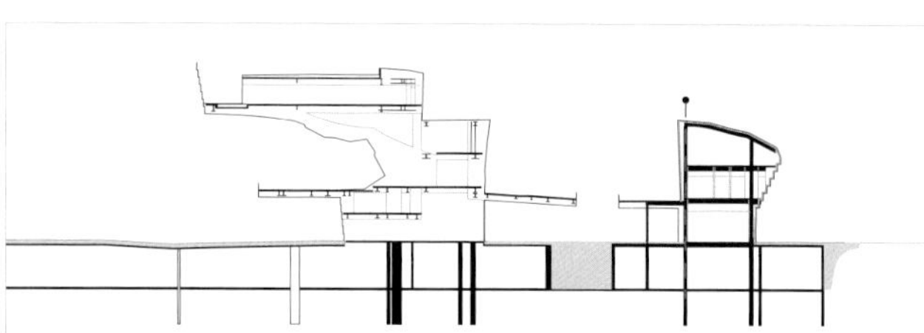

B4

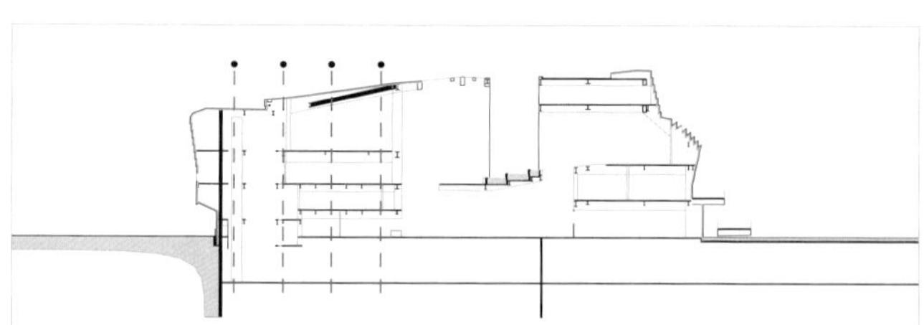

‘So, why did we win? I have asked myself and others many times’

C1

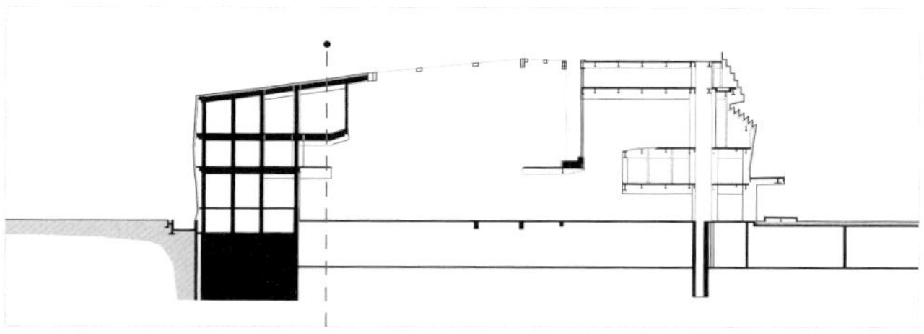

C2

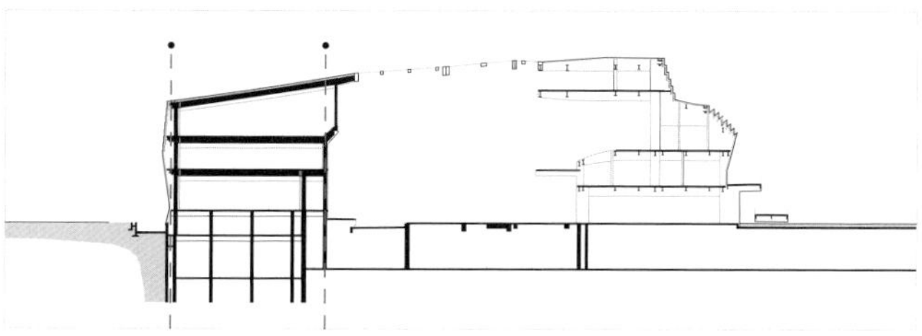

C3

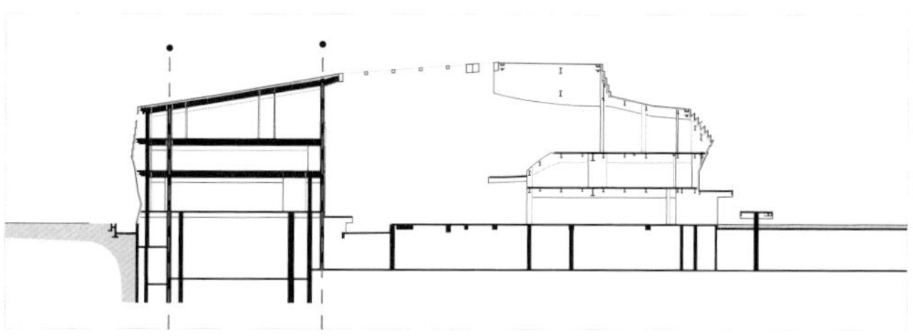

C4

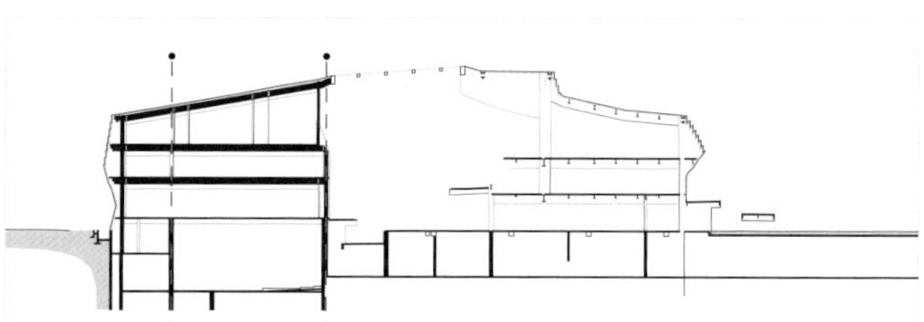

C5

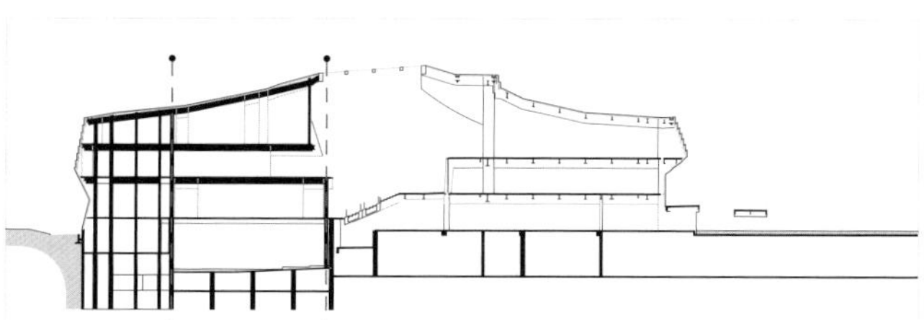

C6

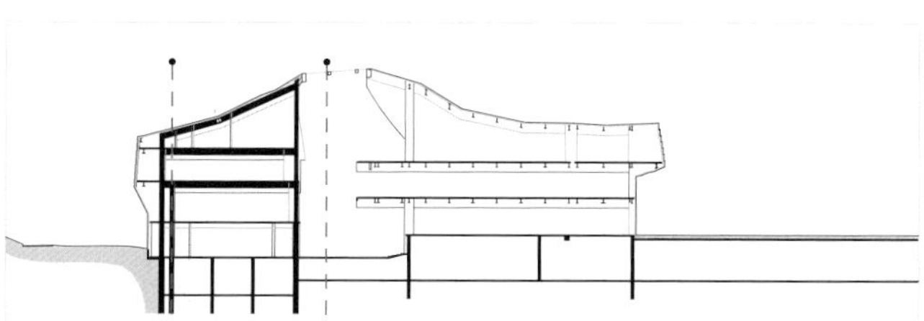

C7

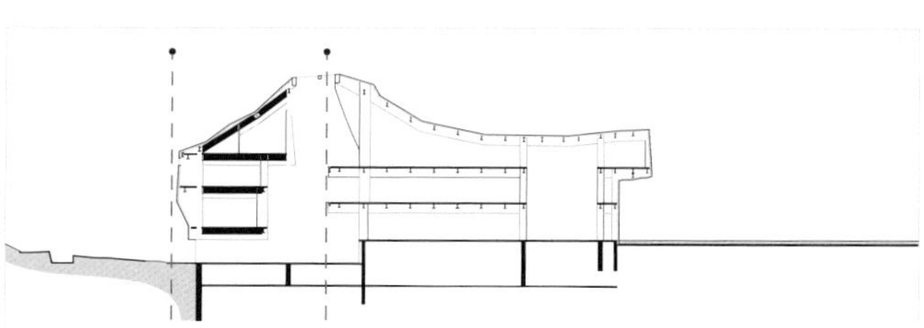

D1

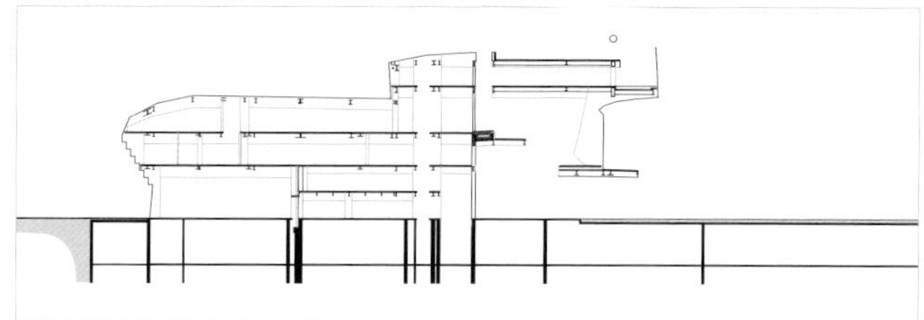

D2

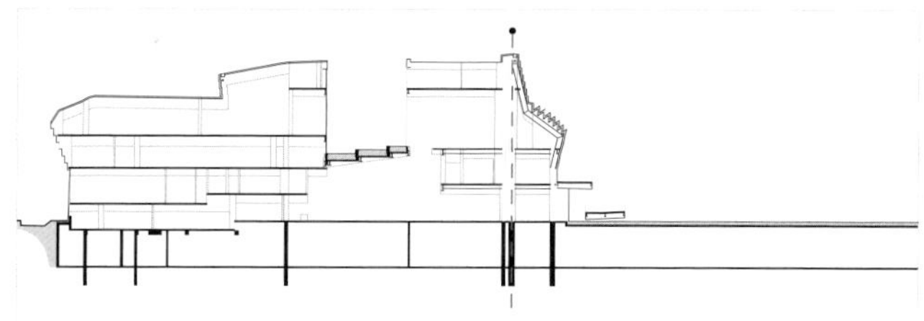

D3

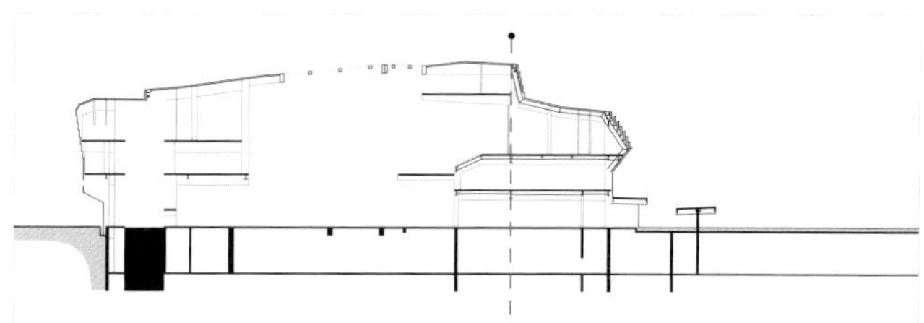

D4

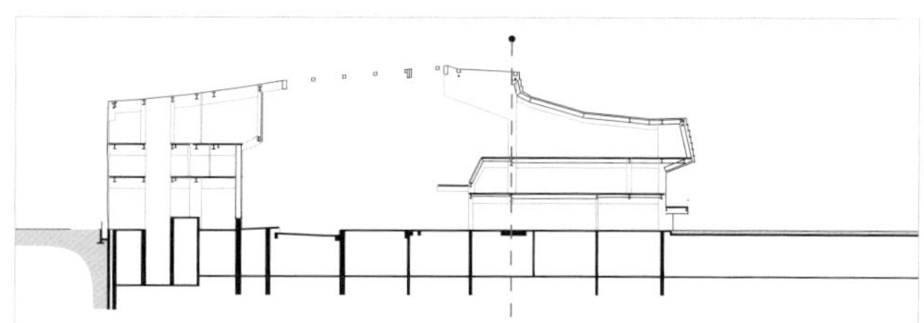

D5

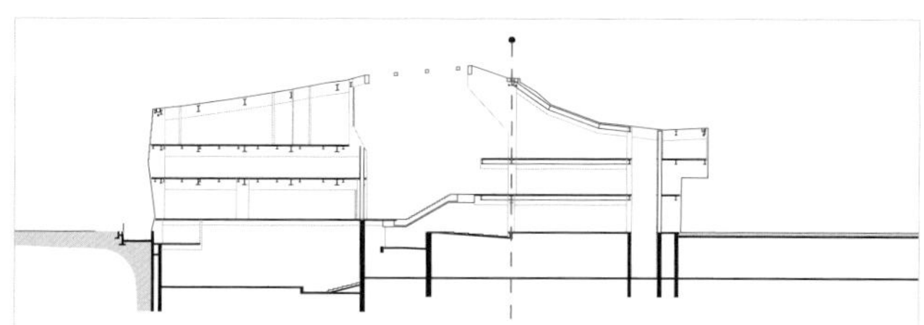

D6

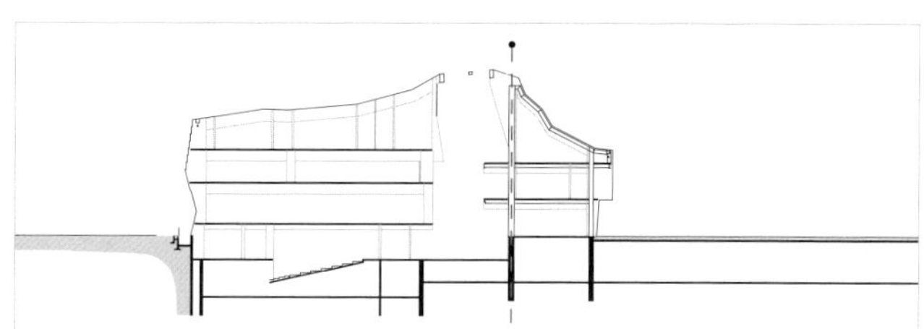

D7

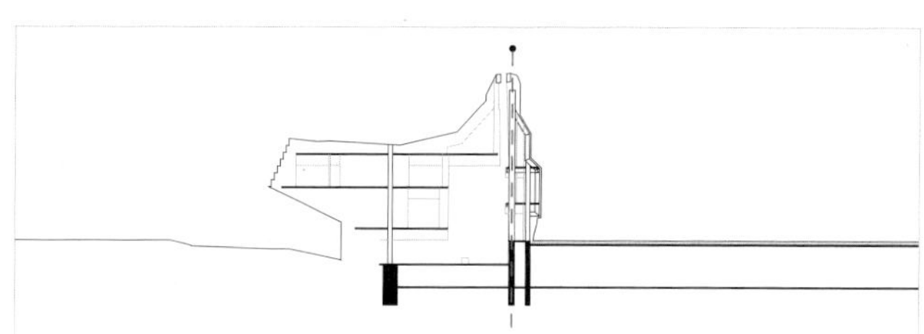

Asher Hartman.
Photo Alexei Tylevich

Text
Katya Tylevich

Domestic Drama

Director Asher Hartman talks about casting architecture for his unusual play.

G

Glass Bang is an experimental musical play written and directed by Asher Hartman, a Los Angeles-based artist and dramatist who makes several meta appearances in the performance. I can't tell you exactly what *Glass Bang* is about, because – in the way that works of art can sometimes be – the play is successfully about a little bit of everything: the banality of life, the claustrophobia of relationships, power struggles, jealousy, self-consciousness and boredom.

Steeped in metaphor, the play follows Gavin (Paul Outlaw) as he startles awake in his home, after a long journey and long stupor, to find it completely redecorated by bickering house-sitters Evan (Michael Morrissey) and Byron (Franc Baliton). Brian (Joe Seely), a Lebowski-like sympathetic 'lowlife' and an apparently uninvited guest, is also making himself comfortable in Gavin's home.

Evan and Byron appear to be in the throes of a marital identity crisis but are nevertheless throwing a party. Surprise! They've invited Gavin's ex-wife, Cheyenne (Rochelle Fabb), and 20 strangers (the audience), including me. Audience members wear nametags (I was 'Cherry') and find themselves in the middle of a party – replete with booze and *amuse-bouche* – which has clearly gone off the deep end. Well, sometimes the only way to deal with a sinking ship (relationship, bank account, identity) is to talk about the design of the cabin. In this case, the cabin is Rudolph Schindler's 1936 Fitzpatrick-Leland House in the Hollywood Hills, in which Hartman staged LA's run of *Glass Bang*.

Throughout the two-hour interactive performance, the home is a stage, a prop, an improvised and scripted distraction, and a strong poetic character. As the home is owned by the MAK Center for Art and Architecture in Los Angeles, and as the performance was a joint venture of The Machine Project Field Guide to LA Architecture project and the Getty's Pacific Standard Time Presents: Modern Architecture in LA initiative, it was hard for this armchair thespian not to make sofa architect observations. After seeing the play, I sat down with Hartman for a coffee and some *Inside the Actor's Studio* hardball: Asher, you've put this play on in different cities; what kinds of homes did you select in each case? To what end? And in Los Angeles, why Schindler? Why modernist architecture? What does it all mean, Asher? →

‘Modernism places value on fairness, but a Schindler house can be accessed only with money’

← **What were your criteria for ‘casting’ a home in *Glass Bang*?**

ASHER HARTMAN: The play is largely a conversation about domesticity and ownership, under the umbrella of class and belonging. Who has the right to be where, and how does architecture host a sense of belonging or rejection? I think that architecture can be a lot like art in the hierarchies of experience that it provides. So in looking for a Los Angeles home, I wanted something that really could be considered ‘art’. To me, that means a home that is beautiful, clear, clean, elegant and, for lack of a better term, upscale. I wanted something that someone might aspire to, but also something that is worth aspiration.

I do feel this Schindler house is a genuine masterpiece. It demonstrates a delicate balance between the outside and the inside and a beautiful synthesis between self, nature and culture. It's also a home in which everybody is visible – you can see into it, and you can look out from it. I knew I wanted a glass home, because of the ways in which that can be very unsettling. This home allows fights to spill out into the front yard. I would say the Fitzpatrick-Leland House is an egalitarian space, or designed as one, but that brings up its own set of issues.

What kinds of issues?

Modernism in general places value on fairness, but this home, like most paintings and art installations, can usually be accessed only with money. So I often think of the strange position of so many artists and of some architects, like Schindler: people with progressive values working in a system that is utterly capitalist. If you want to survive, you work in that system. The Fitzpatrick-Leland House, as well as the play itself, succumbs to this problem. So do I, as an artist and a playwright. I want to talk about social issues within my work. I consider myself political, in some ways, but unless I leave the very system I'm critiquing, I'm always going to be complicit. The tragedy of the play is that of not being able to leave. It's about trying to leave the house but being unable to find your keys – or making it out the door but ultimately coming back, because you need somewhere to live, don't you?

We've been discussing the home in somewhat literal terms, but it's a strong poetic character as well. What symbolism do you attach to it?

I actually think of the single-family home as a metaphor for the body, and that figures heavily in the play. Americans, in particular, have the sense that they have the right to a home. For many, owning a private home means having a body. In the American fantasy, the home is where the nuclear family can grow and exist. Of course, over the last decade it's become evident that the American dream can no longer concentrate on the idea of home ownership. People have had to adjust their definitions of success and their ways of relating to other people outside this structure.

The play's ending is rather blunt, with the actors breaking out of character and casually asking audience members what they think of the housing market.

Oh, yeah, that's an uncomfortable conversation wherever we do the play. It typically breaks down into landlords versus renters, with landlords feeling attacked and renters feeling like they're underwater. It's a simple demonstration of the economic changes we're all going through.

I imagine the Fitzpatrick-Leland House kind of goads the discomfort, since it's not just a single-family home but also, as you say, a work of art – a different kind of status symbol.

It's really more of a museum than just a house. It has an intellectual history, which is atypical of just any single-family house. You can feel energy in the home. You wonder who lived there and who haunts it. To some people, the design might suggest a certain purity, but in fact the home has the residue of many different people, since it's rented out like a hotel or venue. There's a sense of transience in the space, which reflects some of the issues in the play.

The house is available for rent on Boutique Homes, with the caveat that every first Friday of the month it's open to the ‘public by appointment’, and renters need to allow staff and visitors in as part of the rental agreement.

There you go. I bet the renter's idea of a contemplative, private space is disturbed when sightseers come strolling through. [Laughs.] But you know, every home has its own literal, physical presence, which creates a new play every time we move. I do have to change the script and restage the play according to every house we're in.

What are some adjustments you've made?

In Miami, for example, one of the places we used was a mid-century modern home belonging to a wonderful couple with two young children. It generally felt very welcoming and warm in there. For our purposes, we had to consider all the furniture, and I had to rewrite a lot of the script to explain the swing set and children's toys everywhere. These are not things that mesh naturally with the characters. In fact, the Schindler house seems a very unlikely place for children to inhabit. It's almost eerie to imagine. But why? Of course, children could inhabit the home, or did at one point. So maybe that feeling has more to do with the way the house is used now: nobody lives there. Because of that and because of its clean design, it offers a sense of sterility. If a home is a metaphor for the body, then this one is a sterile womb.

Do audience members interact differently inside the Fitzpatrick-Leland House, as opposed to other homes?

Everyone is visible to everybody else, which is important. When an architectural space like this is used as a theatre, it means that at any moment the walls can shift, the energy can shift and audience attention can shift in any number of directions. Our audience is very different from one sitting and looking directly at a proscenium.

I felt a pronounced shift when the actors ran from the main living room into an upstairs bedroom, and the audience, with varying degrees of trepidation, followed the actors into this ‘private’ area, and even onto the bed.

Both the play and the Fitzpatrick-Leland House create a sort of forced intimacy. The actors are the catalysts, of course – they're doing the brunt of the work – but the architecture informs audience members that maybe they're at a party they didn't want to go to, that this is an exciting but awkward situation they're suddenly in. Some members of the audience ease right into it, but others feel the strain of waiting for their ride to arrive and having to make light conversation. The home is something to talk about, in the face of silence. Something like: ‘Oh. This is a nice house.’ ←

asherhartman.com

Glass Bang Stagings

Previous iterations of *Glass Bang* include a non-musical version, called *The Florida Room*, which took place last April in Miami as a co-production of Machine Project (an LA-based non-profit organization committed to arts and social projects) and Cannonball (a Miami non-profit arts organization). The play was staged in two private mid-century modern residences in the MiMo District, a part of town recognized for post-war development known as ‘Miami Modern Architecture’. After its June run in Los Angeles, *Glass Bang* opened in San Francisco as a co-production of Machine Project and Southern Exposure (a Bay Area non-profit that supports visual arts). There, it was staged in a modern home designed by Nilus De Matran.

Glass Bang: A Review

Text **Katya Tylevich**
Photos **Machine Project**

I'm the target audience for an interactive musical play set in one of LA's most name-dropped mid-century modern homes. But I tread lightly into the Fitzpatrick-Leland House for the *Glass Bang* performance, because when you love something (experimental theatre, architecture, your family) you're also more likely to find fault with it and be a critical asshole.

Upon arrival, I feel immediately engaged when audience members are capped at 20, given nametags with new identities and immersed in a staged 'party scene' inside the Schindler house. Booze, appetizers and the home's design serve as icebreakers. The character slumped in a chair throughout this prelude, Gavin, acts as the frozen elephant in the room: nobody within earshot makes reference to him; everyone stays at arm's length. It's the first of many improvised commentaries on how we navigate discomfort in an undefined space.

Eventually, audience members are told to make themselves cosy and to sit facing one another. We try to do as we're told, despite feeling that we've walked onstage not knowing our lines.

In the most literal sense, the play then follows Gavin as he awakes to his house-sitters, Evan and Byron, making a scene over their devolving relationship. Their tug-of-war is between the pragmatic and figurative: Evan is existentially bored, uncomfortable with his ageing body, the routines of coupledom, and the partner who's aged and grown boring beside him. Byron finds intimacy in their shared routines; the sudden break with normality leaves him fatigued and self-conscious.

↑ Heads turn when domestic arguments spill outdoors, and some of the characters end up in the pool.

↓ Characters talk and sing past each other, absorbed by personal issues and unable to make sense of one another's words.

↑ Gavin shares a moment with ex-wife Cheyenne, as he considers his life and how he got to this point.

↓ Brian the barfly slurs through some reasonable observations, as actors and audience members make strange bedfellows.

The couple's increasingly disturbing fight runs parallel to Gavin's frustrations over how they've redecorated his house: neither Gavin's home nor his life resembles his initial designs. The presence of Gavin's ex-wife adds bittersweet salt to his wounds. Meanwhile, a barfly nobody's really invited to the party, comments on the trivial complaints of these people, who seek aesthetic order to overcompensate for their chaotic, jaded inner lives. The play follows characters in their public displays of hospitality and private displays of self-pity. Physical in the tight quarters it creates, *Glass Bang* is otherwise poetic and ethereal, and Hartman's script – offering so much between its lines – is nectar to the literary nerd.

But even the best poetry can be god-awful if delivered improperly. This play relies heavily on talented performances, including those of Hartman himself, who 'disrupts' the play at choice moments to talk his actors off of real and perceived ledges. I'm happy to say that *Glass Bang* is making me embarrassed and uncomfortable for the right reasons: I'm experiencing the rudimentary human anxieties addressed in the play rather than anxiety for its actors, the script or the Schindler house (cast to represent unattained, sometimes superficial aspirations).

Dust covers clean lines, cracks splinter concrete and curtains shroud glass homes. *Glass Bang* is a play about reality falling short of desires. Because I wanted to like this play, I was scared I wouldn't. Well, that makes one anxiety the play puts to rest.

Text
Cathelijne Nuijsink

Photos
Takumi Ota

'Too many architects fail to consider their clients'

Kouichi Kimura is an outspoken Japanese architect inspired by the work of Carlo Scarpa.

← The dead end in the adjacent street ads an extra dimension of surrealism to the strange location and the elongated strip of land.

→ A stairway bathed in light contrasts with dimly lit living areas filled with a warm, subtle glow.

A man in his early 50s, Kouichi Kimura, who founded architecture office Form in 1991, lives and works in Shiga Prefecture, in a town where he happens to be the only architect. Although he admits to having had little contact with architects who run offices in big cities like Tokyo, Osaka, and Hiroshima, he's developed opinions of his own on matters such as the state of contemporary architecture in Japan. A fierce opponent of the DIY approach to education that he believes is prevalent in the country's architecture schools today, he believes students should start by learning the basics of beauty.

For Kimura, beauty is found in the work of Carlo Scarpa (1906-1978), an Italian architect who was, in turn, a great admirer of Japanese art and architecture. Although Kimura has not visited all of Scarpa's projects in person, he has been 'influenced by photographs of Scarpa's work' and, in particular, the Italian's apparent passion for detail. Constructed as an assemblage of surfaces with a Japanese aesthetic, Kimura's latest project, Promenade House, is an ode to the international master.

← Dining area and kitchen, with a view to the entrance hall.

↓ Light entering the interior through small, low windows illuminates the living-room level.

Leftover

In an area where prefabricated houses are the norm and where architects have produced few designs good enough to convince potential clients of their ability to build interesting houses, it takes a certain amount of courage to approach an architect with a request for a family home. In the case of Promenade House, Kimura's clients entered 'architect' and 'Shiga' into an internet search engine, clicked on Kimura's website, and found about 30 custom-designed houses. They had purchased a narrow strip of land, 35 x 4 m, which Kimura describes as 'a cheap leftover spot that had been lying vacant for many years'.

Plans for a site that seemed an unlikely location for a house caused a stir of surprise in the neighbourhood. 'When we start construction in Japan, we have the habit of introducing ourselves to the neighbours,' says Kimura, 'and these people couldn't picture a building of any kind on this narrow strip. Their reaction was: a house next door? Where would you put it?'

In designing the single-family home, Kimura had to consider every centimetre of the property, not just the proportions of the building volume. Unlike a traditional Kyoto town house, for instance, with only its main façade visible to the public, Promenade House pleases the eye when viewed from different perspectives. With its characteristic profile, emphasized by a 3-cm-thick line marking the length of the façade, the dwelling provides passers-by on the walkway to one side of the structure with more than just a boring blind wall.

'You can create a beautiful atmosphere by designing the furnishings as well'

Light

Two skylights and a number of small colourfully framed windows positioned at a relatively low height generate an ambience that combines a Japanese aesthetic with the feel of Le Corbusier's chapel in Ronchamp. By controlling and restricting the amount of natural light that enters the space, Kimura imbues the dimly lit rooms with a warm, subtle glow, which is brightened by vividly coloured window frames.

'When foreigners look at Tadao Ando's architecture, they often describe it as Zen-like, but this house is nothing like that,' says Kimura, referring to Ando's often spiritual expression. To make the most of the window-frame effect, Kimura used high-gloss paint in certain places, for its reflective qualities.

'If this house looks luxurious, it's down to the skilful photography'

→ At the front of the house, the architect opted for a vivid blue-green hallway. He says the colour gives an impression of cleanliness, which carries over to the adjacent bathroom.

↓ At the rear of the house is a double-height study.

Luxury

'If this house looks luxurious, it's down to the skilled work of the photographer, because the project cost less than a prefabricated house,' says Kimura. Why do people in Japan still opt for a prefab model if the price of a custom-designed house is the same? Kimura points to the influence of television, which touts the benefits of prefab until Japanese people believe that nothing is better than owning a ready-made home. He also says that everyone involved in residential design and its implementation should keep in mind the people for whom their buildings are being made. 'Architects sometimes use low budgets as an excuse for eliminating essential things in a house – for the sake of their own concepts. They should do like homebuilding companies do and look at the situation from the occupants' perspective, giving priority to safety measures, for instance, like earthquake-proofing. Too many architects pursue personal dreams or aim for media coverage without considering their clients. I make architecture for my clients, not for myself.'

Closets

Unenthusiastic about the work of young Japanese architects whose bright, open houses result in 'nothing but pulled curtains', Kimura gave his clients a closed volume, stressing what he calls 'the line of flow'. Optimal use of the narrow site meant lining long hallways with rooms, but the interior also offers unexpected turns and a circulation route that is 'not just a straight line'.

Storage space, an aspect of housing design often forgotten by young architects with limited life experience, plays a crucial role at Promenade House. Kimura: 'Architecture is more than design; a house also requires storage space. Even in a house as well organized as this one, you can't have a rich domestic life without good storage space.' The egocentric attitude of many architects annoys him. 'The details I develop are simple and cost little money to produce,' he says, referring to custom-made furniture, hand railings and thick black-leather curtains. 'You can create a beautiful atmosphere by designing furnishings that enhance the interior.'

form-kimura.com

↑ Long hallways give the project its name: Promenade House.

← The circulation route includes not only a staircase at the front of the house but also a ladder at the rear, which connects the two floors and adds another possibility for vertical movement through the interior.

+1

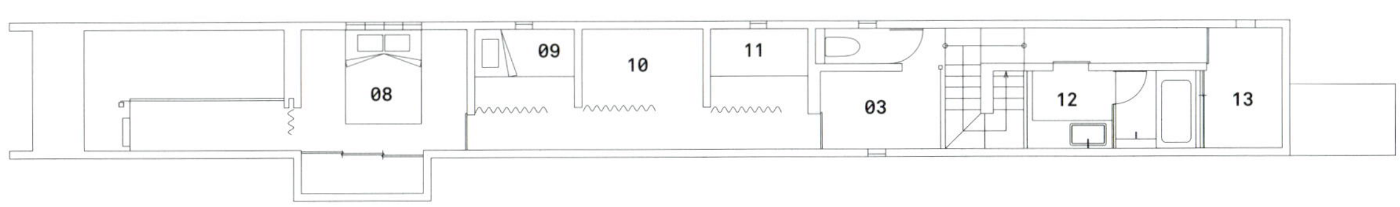

0

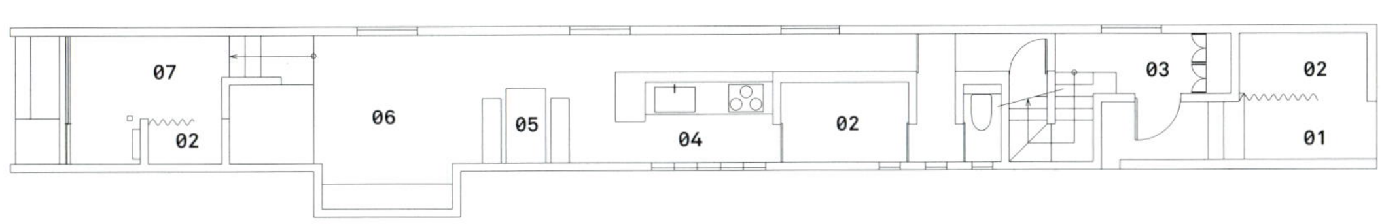

Long Section

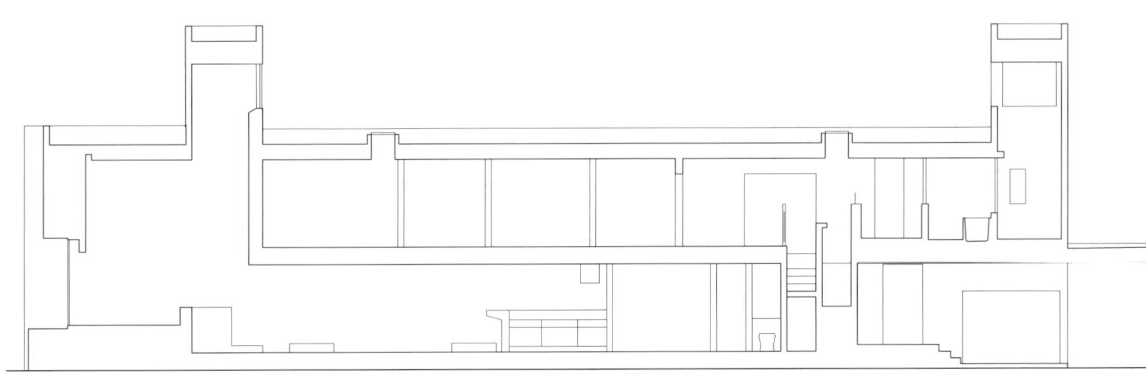

01 Entrance
02 Storage
03 Hall
04 Kitchen
05 Dining area
06 Living area
07 Study
08 Master bedroom
09 Bedroom
10 Walk-in closet
11 Playroom
12 Bathroom
13 Roof terrace

Text
Alexandra Onderwater

Photos
Cristobal Palma

Family Trees

In Lima, 51-1 Arquitectos realized a private residence that snakes among the foliage.

↑ Sightlines play a crucial role in the design – even in the swimming pool.

Y

You'll find a number of inherent conditions in the capital of Peru that are absent in the great majority of the world's metropolises. As an architect, they'll have you champing at the bit. These are qualities you want to capture, use and exploit.

Take the climate, for instance. It never rains in Lima. *Never*? 'Not a drop,' says Manuel de Rivero, who established 51-1 Arquitectos together with César Becerra and Fernando Puente Arnao in 2006. 'It never gets hotter than 28°C or colder than 14°C.' Imagine being an architect working in Lima, and dream scenarios pass before your eyes. Houses without roofs or windows, where outdoors and indoors mesh in seamless harmony. But hold on – have you actually made your way through this dusty city, an urban landscape that's more often than not blanketed in low-hanging clouds, a courteous metonym for 'smog'? And did you notice the highly conspicuous dearth of greenery? 'Green is a luxury in Lima,' says De Rivero. 'Anywhere you see trees or plants, you know they have to be watered.'

'It never gets hotter than 28°C or colder than 14°C'

So when a client drops by your office and talks about wanting to build a house on a parcel of land thick with trees ... you, like any architect worth his salt, are both incredulous and determined to make a go of it. 'We realized immediately that the trees had to stay. What's more, we used them as the point of departure for our design.'

Another unique condition that characterizes Lima: the light. Because the city is so close to the equator, the angle of incidence of the sun's rays is more or less vertical throughout the year. As a result, says De Rivero, 'We don't have to bother with unwanted shadows caused by constantly changing daylight.' Casa Serpiente (Snake House), a residence in an upscale neighbourhood of Lima, was 51-1's second project. Today the firm comprises 21 architects at work on various projects at home and abroad, but on the day they acquired this commission, the three had barely begun their joint venture. Before cofounding 51-1, De Rivero worked in the Netherlands for MVRDV. While his current partners were already knee-deep in 'making', he was concentrating on process description, research and optimal forms of presentation. 'I think it was the way in which we pitched our concept to the clients that ultimately led to us getting the commission for this house. They understood what we wanted to do, even though the means to achieving our goal remained open.' The three became friends at university. 'When we went off to school, everyone called us crazy. Architecture? Can't you study something that offers you a future? In the 1980s and 1990s, Peru was in a deep crisis, →

'Green is a luxury in Lima'

← in more ways than one. It's different now. The economy's advancing in leaps and bounds, and there's so much that still has to be built.' A Valhalla for architects.

The clients, a family, wanted to erect a new house on the very spot where the husband-and-father had lived as a boy. The idea was to convert the existing colonial-style residence into a guesthouse and to build a new, light-filled, contemporary home for the family. 'The funny thing is that our clients looked at the first design, with all its rounded contours, and didn't like what they saw. Curves, they said, were not their thing. And still we got the commission, because we made the 25 trees in their 1,400-m^2 garden the focal point of our design.'

They turned the initial design into a sharply angled snake that slowly, slowly slithers between and along the trees, giving the project its name. Great expanses of fenestration open to the green surroundings, providing occupants with a sense of being in the woods – yet in the very heart of Lima. 'It's quite literally life among the foliage.'

The presence of trees is not the only thing that makes this house different from others in Lima. The typology of Casa Serpiente also deviates from the norm. Instead of rooms arranged around a central courtyard, the 400-m^2 house is a continuous spatial experience. 'Differences in height instil the various internal functions with a kind of rhythm, but what you perceive as you move from room to room is a fluid whole.'

The couple asked 51-1 for separate workplaces. Lisette owns an artisanal flatbread company. Her husband, Irzio, is a restaurateur and entrepreneur. 'From his desk, Irzio can see the tree where his swing hung when he was a child.'

↑ The architects integrated existing trees into their design in such a way that trees have become part of the interior.

There are two ways to access the property. The architects made no changes to the original entrance: a gate next to the existing house. Located at the back of the plot, it is currently referred to as the 'James Bond Entrance': a driveway winds its way to a basement garage large enough for quite a few cars. Also invisible from the street, but in a different way, is the main entrance on the garden side of the house. Once past the high garden wall, however, you receive a whimsical welcome in the form of a timber-clad ramp that leads to the house. This incline features a random pattern of built-in lamps that light up after dark, mimicking the stars in the sky.

The interior is white, light and transparent. 'Connectivity was a basic theme of our design.' This is not a hollow statement. Take the round peepholes in the sides of the swimming pool: a concrete block in the garden. As the children play in the pool, they can duck underwater and wave through the holes to their dad in his study. And then you have a pair of mature trees growing out of the ground and straight into the house. The most remarkable is the glass-encased white cedar (*Melia azedarach*) in the living room. Two walls enclosing this tree are made from mirrored glass. 'The outcome is an alienating, rather kaleidoscopic effect,' says De Rivero. It's as if the presence of trees in this extraordinary project hasn't been emphasized enough in the design of the house. Nearly all rooms have windows that face the garden. And from virtually every spot you have contact with people elsewhere in the house. The open-plan kitchen can be described as a 'fully glazed box'. At Casa Serpiente, preparing dinner is seldom done in isolation.

The climate permits the most minimal of separation between inside and outside. Open stairwell, single-glass windows, semi-covered walkway – not a problem in Lima. According to De Rivero, the city's weather conditions all but guarantee sustainability. A situation that would tempt many an architect to sell his soul. ←

51-1.com

↑ Exterior walls of brick and concrete are clad in Graniplast, a continuous acrylic-polymer coating.

→ White epoxy floors unify the winding structure, while bright colours – such as the orangey red of the sunken sitting area in the playroom – add cheerful accents to the interior.

Old

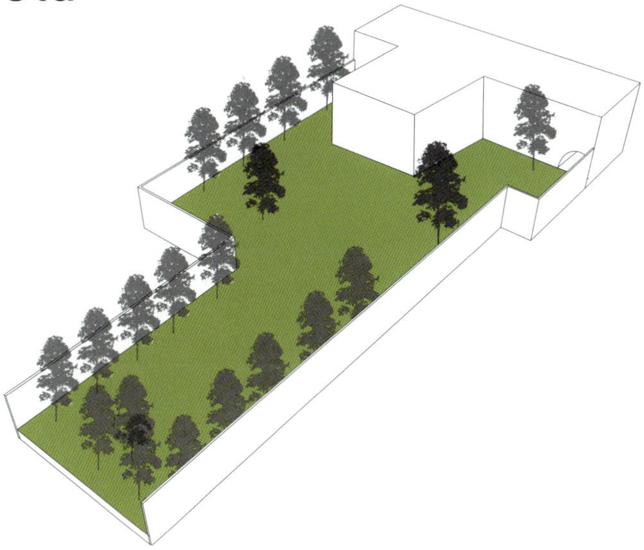

New

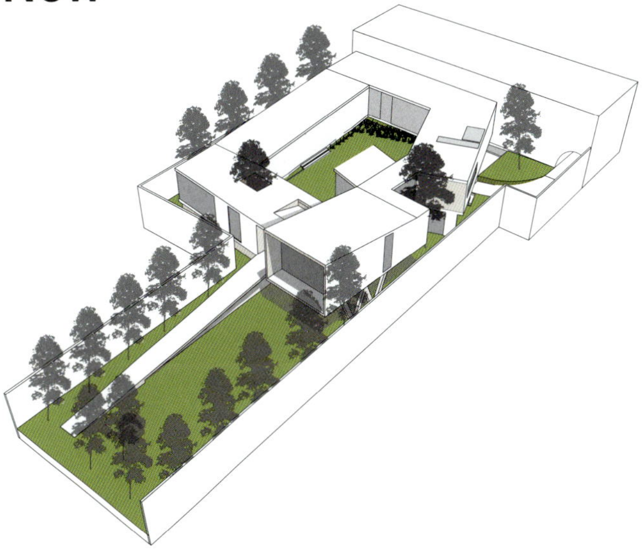

Long Section

→ Mirrored-glass walls around the white cedar (*Melia azedarach*) create a kaleidoscopic effect.

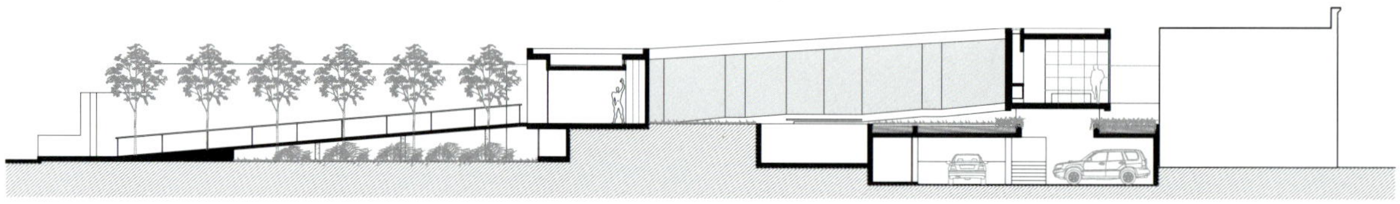

+1

01 Main entrance
02 Driveway ('James Bond Entrance')
03 Garden
04 Covered garden
05 Study
06 Garage
07 Gym
08 Staff bedroom
09 Staff living room
10 Existing house
11 Entrance hall
12 Living room
13 Dining room
14 Extra kitchen
15 Main kitchen
16 Laundry
17 Walk-in closet
18 Bathroom
19 Master bedroom
20 Bedroom
21 Playroom
22 Pool

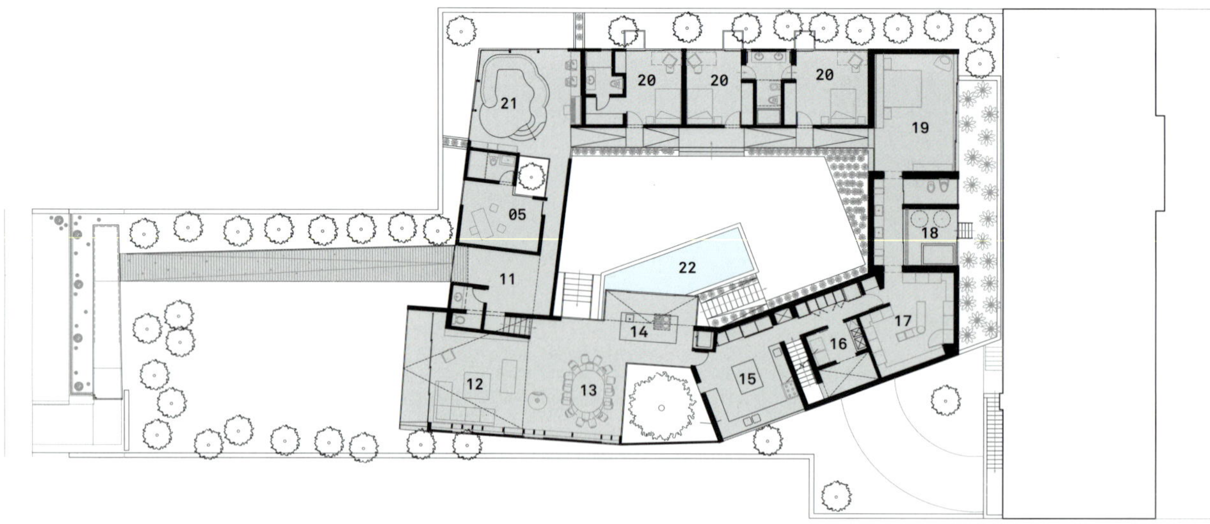

0

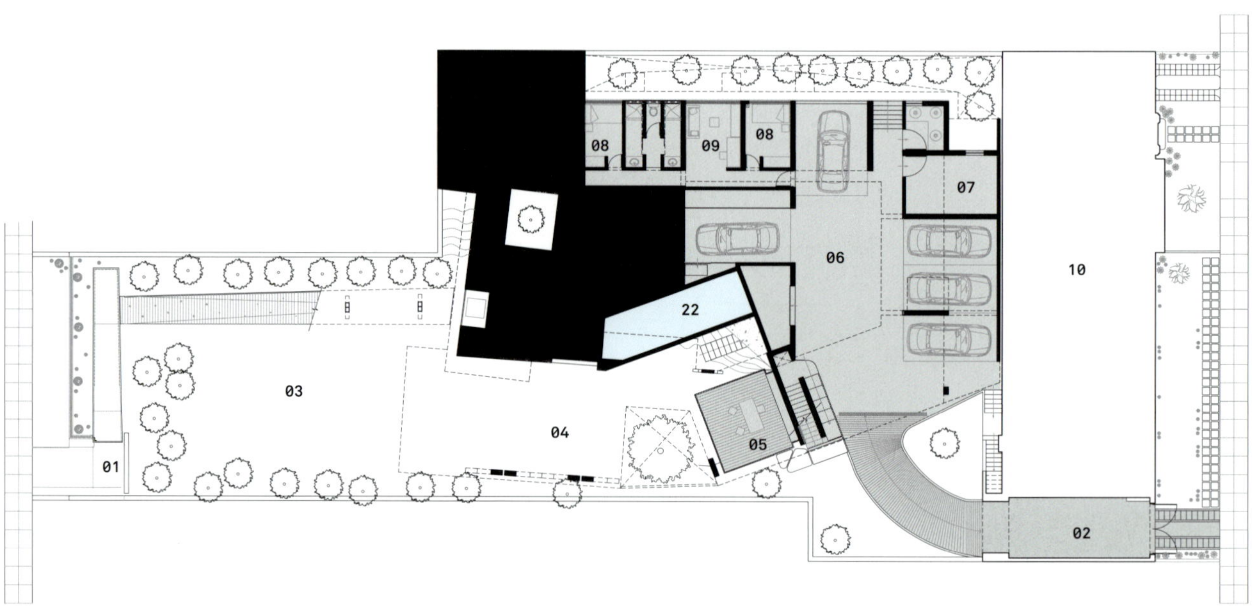

An Architect's Playground

Helle Schröder and Martin Janekovic designed a house for themselves that flies in the face of every architecture convention imaginable.

Text
Florian Heilmeyer

Photos
Anja Büchner

← The ground floor accommodates areas for storage, work and play. Unlike many of the houses in this small neighbourhood, this one has no cellar.

↓ A net hangs in the void to prevent a fall that might cause injury. Schröder doesn't like railings and balustrades.

I've been in this house for more than three hours now, and I'm still discovering something new at every turn. We go upstairs, traipse back down, scale another flight of steps, climb a ramp – constantly ascending and descending in a house that consists mainly of stairways. Only when we reach the roof terrace, a spot that emphasizes the exceptional location of this house, does my view turn outward again. Visible to the south is the gleaming silver orb of the Fernsehturm (TV tower), and in the opposite direction a sightline through the kitchen reveals the Berlin Wall Memorial at Bernauer Straße. Where only a couple of decades ago the infamous 'death strip' divided the city in two, tourists stroll, point and wave – at us. 'Above all else, architecture should be fun,' says architect Helle Schröder.

Sounds great – but how does it work? And how does it work in this of all places? From time immemorial, architecture has been serious business in Berlin, and Schröder's house occupies an emotionally charged site. Every day the house is viewed and photographed by hundreds of tourists, because it is part of a tiny neighbourhood of 16 individually designed and very modern town houses that mark the line once followed by a menacing wall that severed two Berlin boroughs: Mitte and Wedding. It looks rather strange – this tight cluster of houses on a slight rise, overlooking the city – especially in light of all the land around them, surely enough to have allowed them to spread out a bit. These dwellings have an urban-planning oversight to thank for their privileged location. After the wall was torn down, this area, like so many others in Berlin, was seen as part of a historical city plan that had to be reinstated. Large housing blocks were to be erected along the street, with town houses in the courtyards behind them. Local politicians wanted to turn the fragmented city into a coherent whole as rapidly as possible, particularly those peripheral inner-city areas that had been left vacant after the wall was demolished. Fortunately, such plans were never fully implemented.

The loss that these barbaric plans from the '90s would have meant to the city is clearly visible today. The Berlin Wall Memorial consists of an open strip of land that follows the trajectory of the wall. The location of the wall itself is indicated by slender steel poles positioned at some distance from one another. Outlined on the ground are parts of a watchtower and the course of a few escape tunnels – poignant reminders of a dark but crucial era in the history of Berlin.

All of which adds up to a small group of dwellings in an enviable spot. The memorial next door ensures the occupants of an unobstructed view, indefinitely, at a very central location. Okay, what they get in exchange for that view is hordes of tourists, 'but only from nine to five', says Schröder. 'We got used to it very quickly. In the evening, things settle down and kids play football, often on the memorial lawn.' At such moments, what she sees is her private sliver of the wall.

'We just got lucky,' she says, 'because plans for this little neighbourhood were already in the works when someone came up with an idea for a memorial.' Designs for the façades of the houses – after the plans were changed, this was the only →

'Above all else, architecture should be fun'

← new-build project that would border this stretch of the wall – had to take the memorial into consideration. Materials seen as 'too cheerful', such as wood or stucco, were not permitted; a German memorial to the Third Reich or the Berlin Wall cannot be frivolous: it's got to be built of steel or concrete.

In line with the brief, therefore, the house that Helle Schröder and Martin Janekovic designed for themselves and their two children has a rather cool exterior with large windows framed in black aluminium and dark steel. The remarkable half-timbered look and the whimsical tie-down straps dangling from the façade, which are meant to heighten privacy and sway lightly in the breeze, are the first indications of a strong concept that has been carried out with humour and elegance. Architecture can indeed be fun, even here, next to what was once a formidable barrier.

'We had only a 118-m^2 site to work with,' says Schröder, 'which is not only relatively small; this plot is also a trapezium. Our first decision was to completely open the exterior walls that face north and south. We wanted a house filled with as much natural light as possible.' Daylight needed to enter the house from above as well; consequently, they treated the interior – 5 x 8 x 12.6 m – as a continuous space, largely without separate rooms.

'Floor plans have never interested me very much anyway,' says Schröder. 'They've always seemed like a completely inadequate means of depicting a room.' In this case, Schröder and Janekovic took the sectional plane as their point of departure, worked with models and ultimately designed a diagonal sequence of open zones that traverse the entire interior. They included only two closed volumes, which 'hang' in the space and accommodate lockable bedrooms. All other areas merge to form one uninterrupted space that spans no fewer than seven levels, from the ground floor to the very top of the house. These levels are connected to one another by stairs, footbridges and ramps.

This arrangement creates an astonishing sense of space. As you move through the interior, new sightlines open up in every direction. You experience not one moment of claustrophobia. Occasionally, long sightlines combined with verticality evoke a →

→ The bath tub is in the middle of the living area, with only a curtain for privacy.

↓ Behind a slanting concrete wall is the master bedroom, accessible via a footbridge.

'I like houses based on a strong concept, but not when it becomes a dogma'

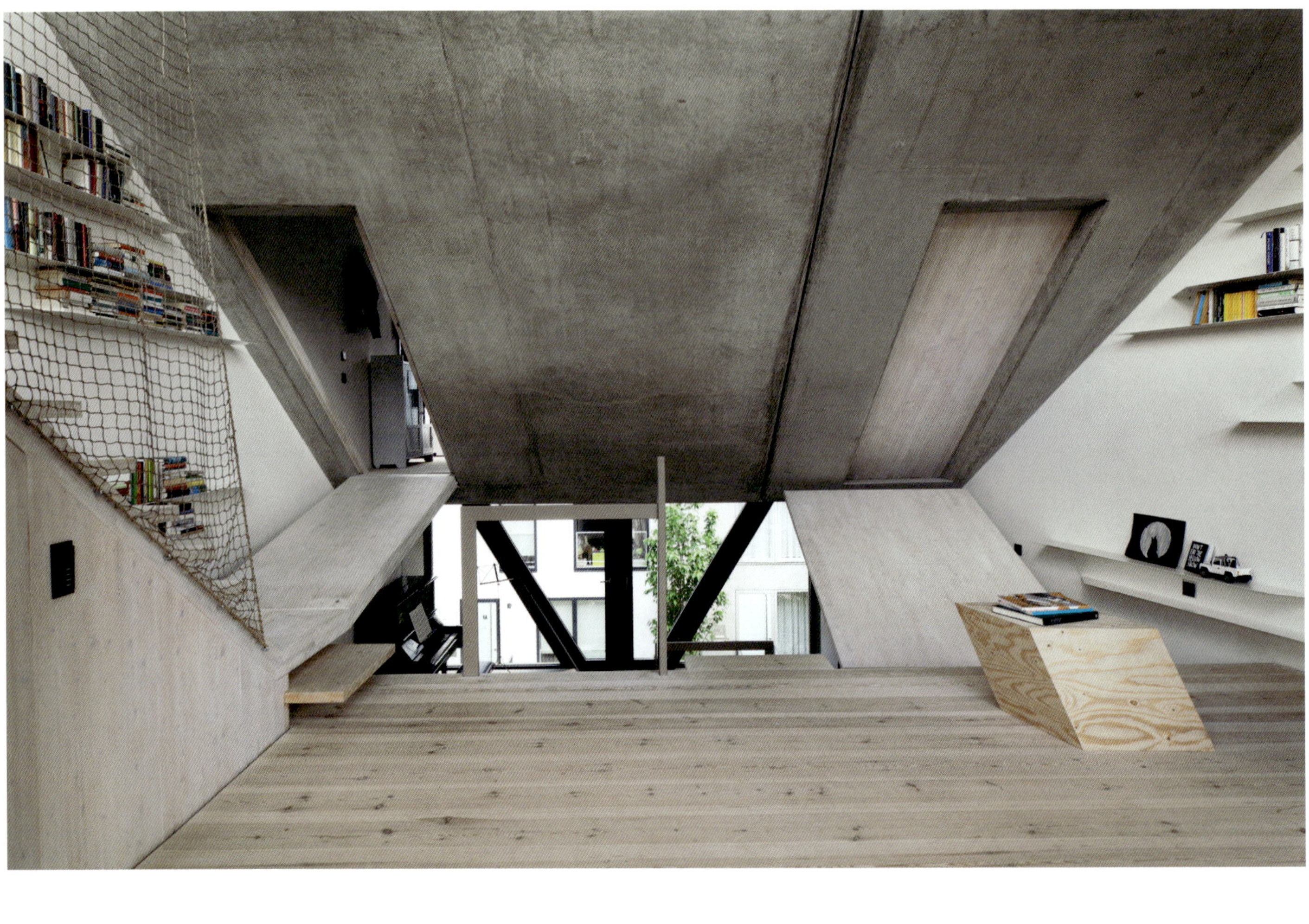

House → Berlin | Germany

← Helle Schröder and her daughter Liva in the living area.

→ With the hatches closed, the children have cosy quarters that offer a sense of privacy.

↘ Separate bedrooms for the two children, Liva (13) and Dan (11), occupy the first floor. These bedrooms have conventional doors as well as large hatches and a ramp.

'The house reminds some people of the mountains, a boat or a spaceship'

← sense of climbing a mountain path that constantly turns in yet another direction – a feeling underpinned by a series of nets installed throughout the house to prevent falls that might cause injury.

Helle Schröder laughs when I mention hiking in the hills. 'All these ramps do seem to make some people think of mountain paths, but others compare the house to a boat or even a spaceship. While we were designing the house, we weren't trying to evoke any kind of image at all. Our only goal was the realization of a continuous, well-functioning space.' A concept based on sloping floors and stairs did rob them of a certain amount of floor area, though, but Schröder isn't bothered. 'We had to deal with all sorts of arguments against our concept. Most banks, in particular, proved to have very little imagination, recognizing only "reduced value" in a design that deviated from the norm. We realized from the word go that our house would have a few less square metres, but we didn't see that as a loss. On the contrary, we feel as if our design has provided us with *more* room.'

She doesn't need an explanation to convince *me*. I've just taken the tour and am still overwhelmed by the power of the place. It's amazing how harmonious the interior is despite all the ramps and stairs – thanks in part to a limited palette of materials and colours: concrete, whitewashed wood and beige steel. Coherence also emerges from the architects' application of a 35.5-degree angle for nearly every incline, which is the angle used for a fairly normal flight of stairs.

'In general, I like houses based on a strong concept,' says Schröder, 'but not when it becomes a dogma to which everything is forced to conform.' Steering well clear of a 'dogma', the architects decided not to use the same angle for furnishings, floors and the half-timbered pattern in the façade. It is precisely the use of small, attractive discrepancies that give this house its air of maturity. It is not a meticulously detailed design object, but an adaptable and thus livable space.

'We couldn't be sure, of course, that everything would turn out as expected in our day-to-day use of the space,' says Schröder. 'For example, we installed curtain rods above all the windows, thinking we might get tired of being on display all the time and want to hang curtains. We've been here nearly a year now, and I still like it the way it is. When tourists wave at us, we just wave back. The house is kind of like a playground. I enjoy every day here. Stacking rooms on top of each other is boring. Our home functions differently; it transcends the conventions of the floor plan.' ←

xth-berlin.de

+3

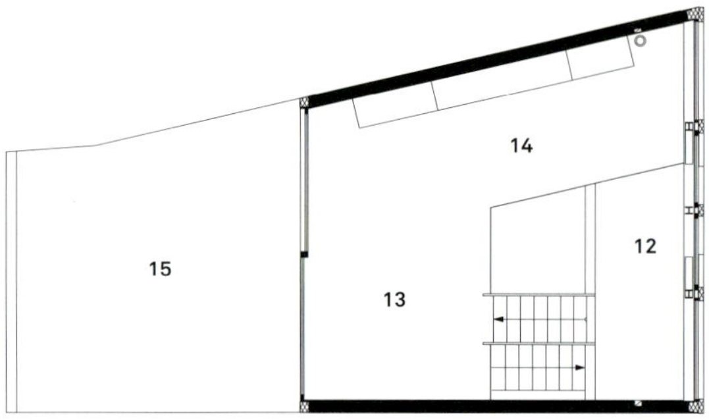

+2

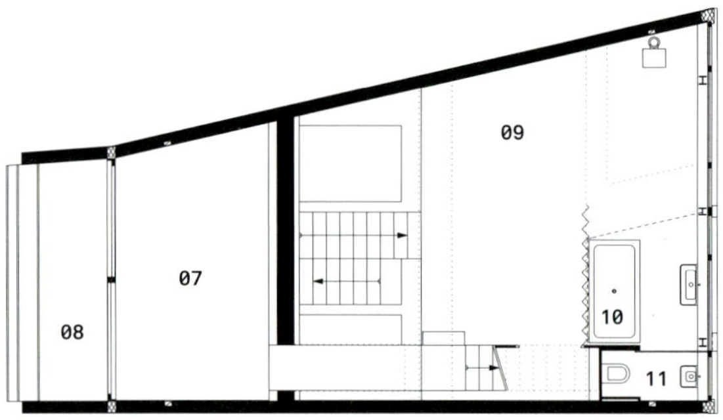

+1

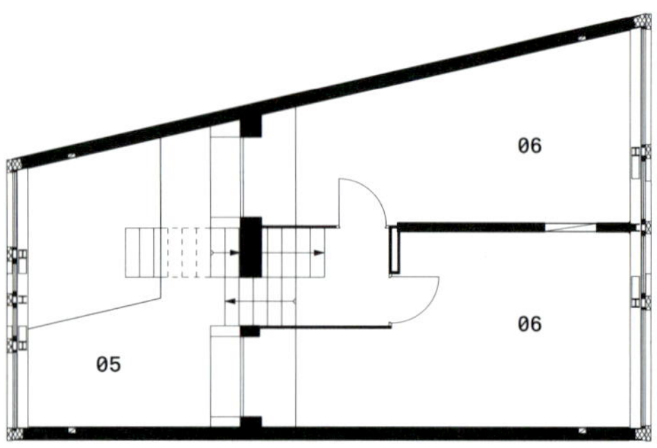

0

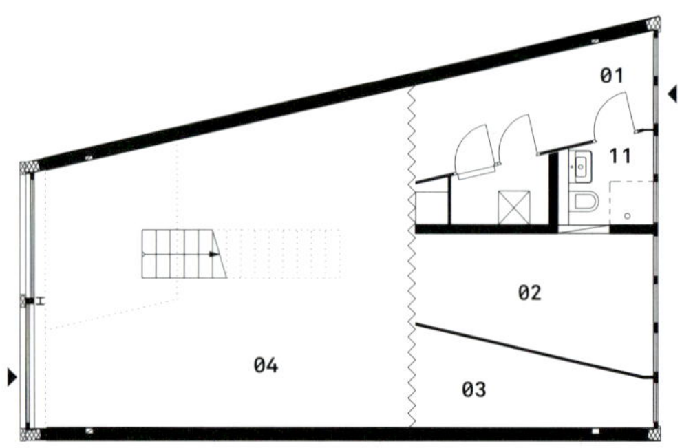

01 Entrance hall
02 Guest bedroom
03 Study
04 Foosball and workspace
05 Music area
06 Children's bedrooms
07 Master bedroom
08 Balcony
09 Living area
10 Bath tub
11 Toilet
12 Reading area
13 Dining area
14 Kitchen
15 Roof terrace

'Floor plans have never interested me very much'

Long Section

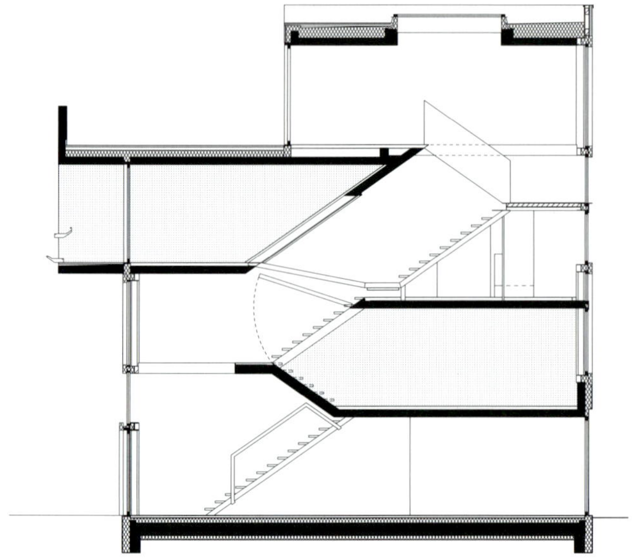

Perspective

Site Plan

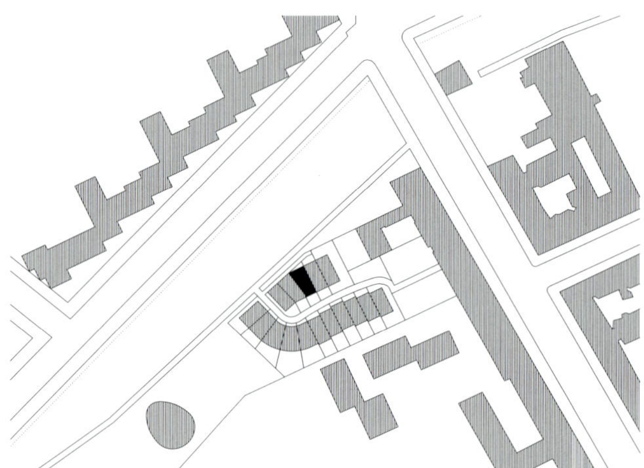

On the top floor is the kitchen, which opens to the roof terrace. Like a mountaintop, the light-filled space offers long views of the levels below.

Text
Bert de Muynck

‘Design starts with an understanding of your resources’

Hua Li of TAO uses local construction techniques to build in remote places.

It is a typical grey summer day in Beijing, and I am walking around Chaochangdi Village in the northeast part of town. Known locally as 'Ai Weiwei Village', for the notorious Chinese artist who lives nearby, this area looks like a cross between a rural habitat and a haven for artists. Ai Weiwei's grand and monolithic red and grey structures – housing artists' studios and offices – contrast with buildings quickly erected by the local population. In recent years, artists, galleries and architects have moved into the area and set up somewhat of a creative community of their own. One of these architects is Hua Li, who founded TAO (Trace Architecture Office) in 2009. His ambition was to explore 'a sense of place; a response to climate, material and construction methods; and an efficient use of resources'.

TAO is one of those smaller-scale Chinese outfits that possess an intriguing ability to operate on the fringes of urban, rural and regional architecture, thus creating an approach and a language that in each case bears a unique signature. TAO's projects and their locations 'still have diversity and are not yet globalized', according to Hua, but they do reveal 'traces of local materials and construction techniques'.

One example is the Xiaoquan Elementary School in Sichuan Province – a response to the Sichuan earthquake of 2008 that severely damaged many structures in the area. With donations from the Red Cross and others, TAO built a new school in the centre of Xiaoquan Old Town, conceived as a cluster of small buildings that form a micro city-like campus. The architects relied not only on the know-how of local craftsmen, but also on local bricks, wood, bamboo and concrete.

Currently, TAO has two projects in the construction phase: one in Guangzhou, an 8,000-m^2 children's hospital, and one in Sichuan, a kindergarten and art school. In spite of the great demand for architects in China, Hua wants to keep his studio small. 'Right now there are eight people working here, and we do not have interns,' he says. 'We have two projects in the design process and two others under construction. I do not like to do too many things at the same time. If you have too many things to do, you do not have enough time to concentrate.'

Other projects, such as the Bamboo Raft Factory in the Wuyishan Mountains (Fujian Province) and the Museum of Handcraft Paper at the foot of Gaoligong Mountain (Yunnan Province), exemplify Hua's wish 'to work on small-scale projects, allowing me more time for design and a better control of the building process'. For architects operating from China's capital, it can be hard to keep control over projects they have designed for locations in the countryside. Hua confesses, however, that his desire for control and a straightforward approach can also lead to conflicts: 'The Bamboo Raft Factory in Fujian is nearing the start of construction and faces a lot of challenges from an organizational perspective. The way it works is that they first need to burn the bamboo so they can bend it, and once this is done they need to assemble it quickly with wires. While this is going on, there's continuous fire and smoke at the building site, which not everybody involved finds a good idea.'

Striking a balance between form and construction technique is an important part of TAO's projects in remote places, but the firm has also been developing a series of urban buildings with a more modern style. The Riverside Clubhouse in Yancheng is a sort of folded Farnsworth House, for which TAO created a new form by stretching, looping and folding Mies's famed design. The viewing pavilion on a hill in Tashan Park in Weihai is conceived as a half-buried, half-cantilevered volume with three viewing platforms spread out like the branches of a tree. In his design, Hua focused on incorporating existing trees on the site into the project, but, as always, 'during construction some careless workers destroyed a couple of trees'.

As it happens, Hua has just come back from visiting the Xiaoquan Elementary School over the weekend. He pulls out his mobile phone and shows me some images. 'I like to see how the children are using the space and playing in it,' he says. 'These children have their own way of using the space, which is different from the way I thought about it during the design phase. Users are always very creative.'

The architects incorporated existing trees into the design.

Viewing Pavilion on Hill

Weihai | Shandong | China | 2012

TAO realized a pavilion on a woodland hillside in Tashan Park, which is part of Weihai, a coastal city in Shandong Province. To protect existing trees and to offer a view of the city's major sights, the architects designed a partially sunken building that includes three branchlike viewing tubes which face different points of interest. The pavilion provides visitors with experiences on two levels. Walking down half a level, you enter a tearoom and gallery with framed views of outdoor vistas. The roof terrace affords a breathtaking panoramic view over the Yellow Sea.

Photos Yao Li

← The pavilion is half buried and half cantilevered.

↓ The roof of the pavilion offers a view over the Yellow Sea.

‘Remote places force us to go back to the fundamentals of our profession’

Long Section

01 Main entrance
02 Tearoom
03 Gallery
04 Terrace
05 Secondary entrance
06 Office
07 Monitoring room
08 Women's rest room
09 Men's rest room
10 Utility room
11 Equipment room

+1

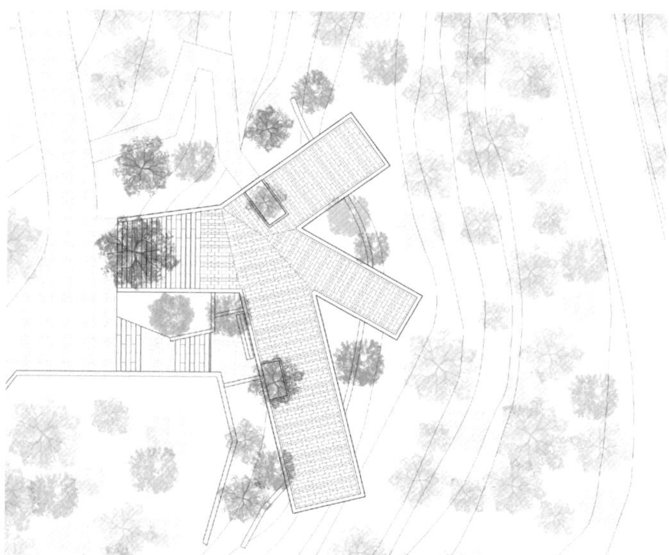

0

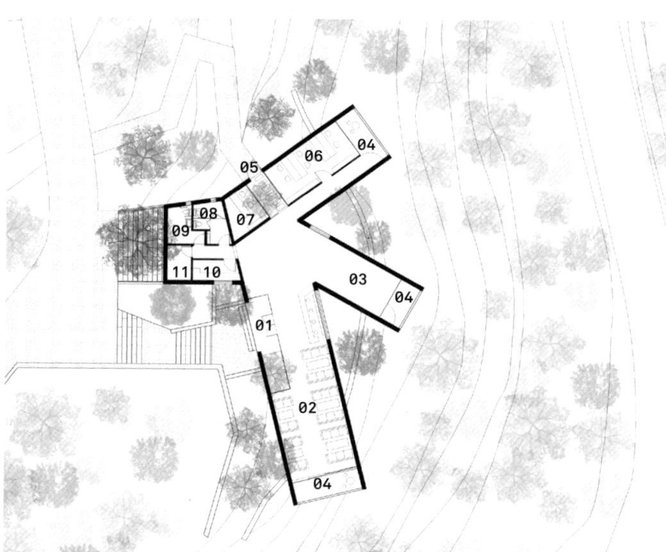

What surprised you when you saw the children at the Xiaoquan Elementary School? Can you give an example?

HUA LI: We designed a small corner space for the children, with benches in concrete, but they are using them as tables to do their homework. I even saw a kid using a bench to do sit-ups. Another element of our design – which we call 'window furniture', meant for children to sit or lie down in – has been turned into a small outdoor library. When you return to projects and observe their use, it helps you to understand how the place adapts to daily activities. I rarely do commercial projects initiated by developers, projects where you do not know who the user is. When a client asks me to design something first – for users to be determined later – I simply say no. Look at all these museum projects in China. They ask you to design one without even know what they're going to put in it. This is very common and quite ridiculous, if you think about it.

Does it demand another way of looking at architecture?

I am interested in projects that have a clear typology, where you can define how the place will be used. This is important, as a lot of projects are very ambiguous in their programme, especially in China. When you face the uncertainty of the market, architecture is very difficult to conceive. I do not believe in this so-called 'flexibility', as it often means nothing. I prefer specificity.

Your recent projects have been constructed in remote places in China. On the subject of specificity, it is also important to understand the construction process behind such projects. How do you make sure people deliver what you want? Can you talk about that process?

I believe a design starts with an understanding of the resources you have at your disposal, as this becomes part of your ideas regarding the construction and use of material. A good example is the Museum of Handcraft Paper, located in a village that is an enclosed system. It is not like a big city, where you can use whatever you want if you have the money. Our first aim was to realize a contemporary building rooted in the local condition, and to do this we needed to learn about and understand traditional Chinese timber structures. It was important to have a local building team involved and to use the resources at hand.

But how do villagers react to your architecture? It must be difficult to introduce a new architectural language into a village. Is there resistance among local people, or do they think it's fantastic?

Some people think my buildings are a bit strange, of course, as they differ from local examples. What we do is something of a marriage; I use that word when talking with villagers. It connects them with outsiders, people drawn to the area to find out more about the paper-making tradition. A new museum has the potential to transform the economy of a village and the lifestyle of those living there. But this project was also about the development of traditional timber techniques. The local construction team we worked with explained that the system they use is highly adaptable, for making not only traditional, symmetrical designs but also those based on other languages of form. It is important for builders to know they can go beyond the norm and can apply the same methods to different projects.

You were born in Gansu, one of the smallest and most underdeveloped provinces in China. Did growing up there influence your way of looking at and thinking about architecture?

If it's true that your childhood environment has a certain impact on you, then mine may have had an impact on me. Professor Raimund Abraham of the Cooper Union was a good friend of mine. He once said, 'Hua Li, you are a peasant, and so am I.' It's part of my personality. I do not like things to be theoretical, but more down to earth. Gansu is a very traditional region and has, unlike what you find in cities, a provincial culture. People are simple; food is authentic. I grew up in that environment and it must have influenced me. Maybe that's why I prefer to do projects in remote places with bare circumstances, which force us to go back to the fundamentals of our profession and forget about formalistic or fancy design.

Is it important for you to define your style? The elements I see in your work run the gamut from local and regional to critical and modernist.

I do not have a style, and I do not want to be defined by any style.

Is this a good moment to be an architect in China?

A good moment? It is hard to say when it's a good moment to be an architect. What I can say is that it's always torture. ←

t-a-o.cn

Museum of Handcraft Paper

Gaoligong Mountain | Yunnan | China | 2010

The museum is close to a village in southwest China, at the foot of Gaoligong Mountain, a national nature reserve that enjoys the protection of the WWF and UNESCO. Besides exhibiting the history and culture of paper-making, which has strong traditional roots in the village, the museum includes a book store, an office and guest rooms. The architects chose local *sha* wood for both structural elements and finishes. The framework features traditional columns and beams without nails, the so-called *sun and mao* system, which was executed skilfully by local builders. Bamboo was used as a roofing material.

Photos Shu He

01 Entrance hall
02 Gallery
03 Tearoom
04 Book shop
05 Kitchen
06 Storage
07 Courtyard
08 Work area
09 Meeting room / reception
10 Void
11 Guest room
12 Roof terrace
13 Lounge

+2

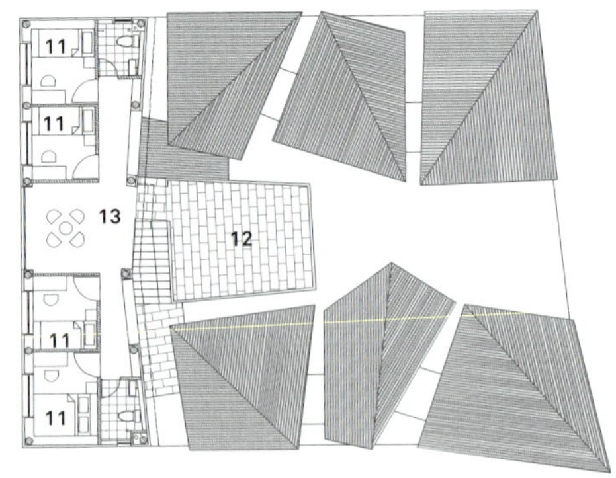

+1

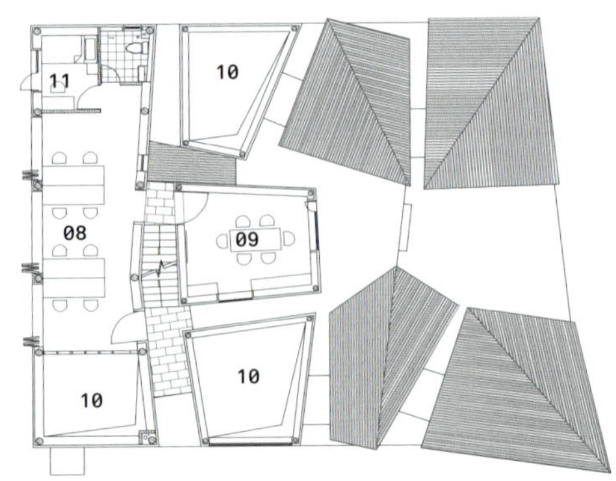

0

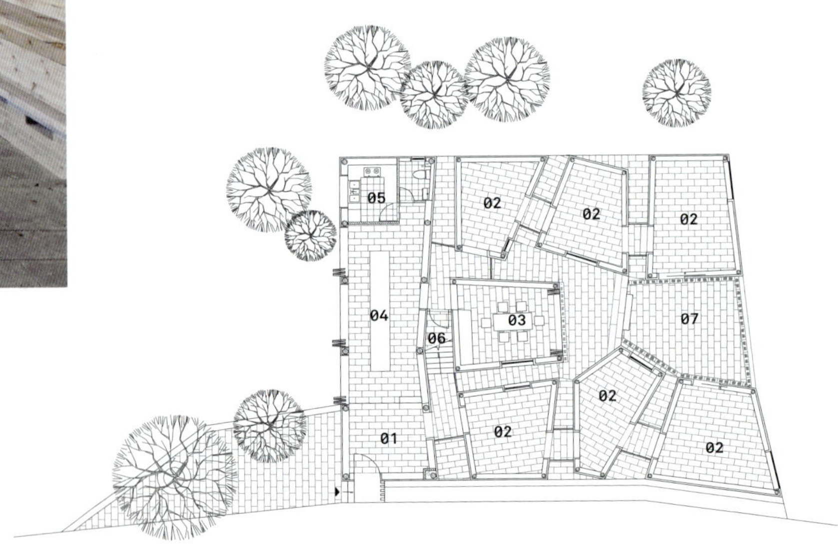

Long Section

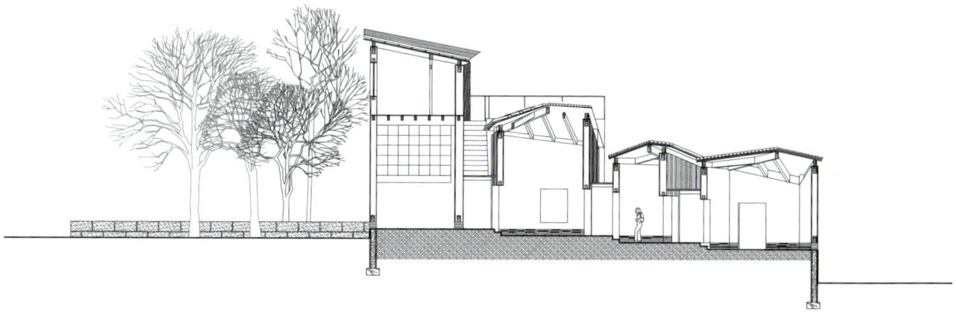

↑ The museum complex was conceived as a micro-village, a cluster of several small buildings.

← With the exhibits in place, the museum highlights the history and culture of paper-making.

↓ Walking through the museum, visitors experience an alternating pattern of interior gallery spaces and outdoor areas.

Riverside Clubhouse

Yancheng | Jiangsu | China | 2010

On the north bank of a small river, surrounded by a park and a sports field, is the Riverside Clubhouse. During the design phase, Hua Li took as his starting point Mies van der Rohe's Farnsworth House, stretching, looping, folding and ultimately transforming it. Results include a reduced building depth that affords excellent views, a courtyard that offers privacy, an accessible roof terrace, and close proximity to the water. Low-iron glass, white aluminium panels, travertine floors, precast concrete panels and transparent glass partitions create the desired abstract atmosphere.

Photos Yao Li

+ 1.80 m

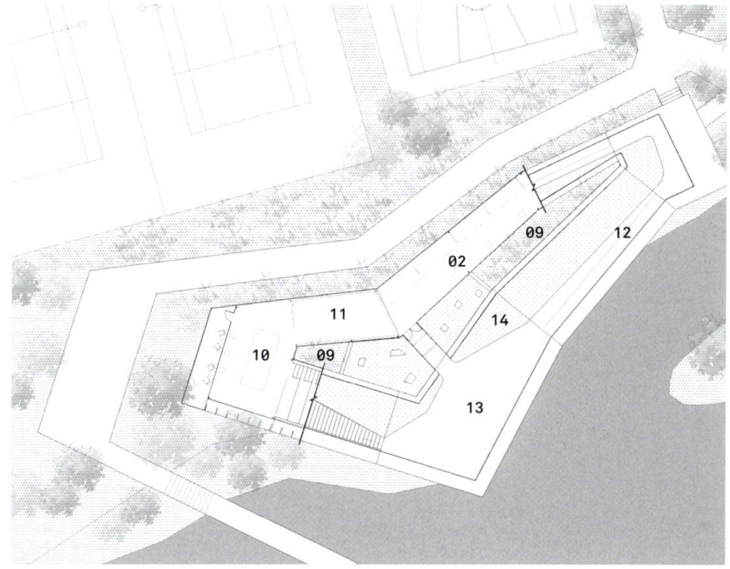

Section

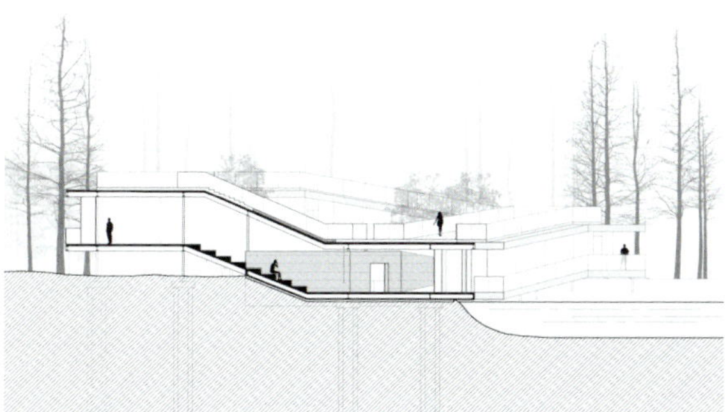

0

01 Lobby
02 Gallery
03 Meeting room
04 Children's room
05 Lounge
06 Bar
07 Office
08 Auditorium
09 Courtyard
10 Exhibition
11 Video area
12 Walkway
13 Roof terrace
14 Green roof

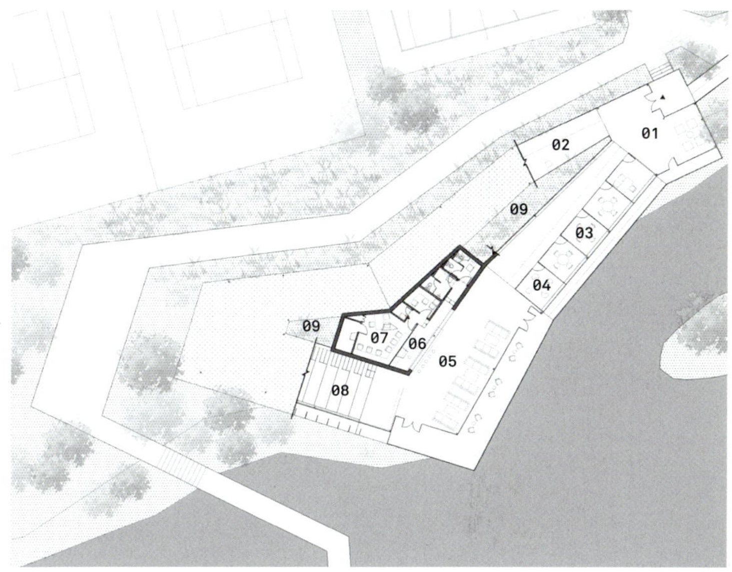

↑ The architects tackled the problem of soft soil by placing columns on a pile foundation, a solution that makes the building seem to hover above the ground.

← Abundant use of glass resulted in a transparent building.

→ The design incorporates a 2-m change in level between river and building site.

Axonometric

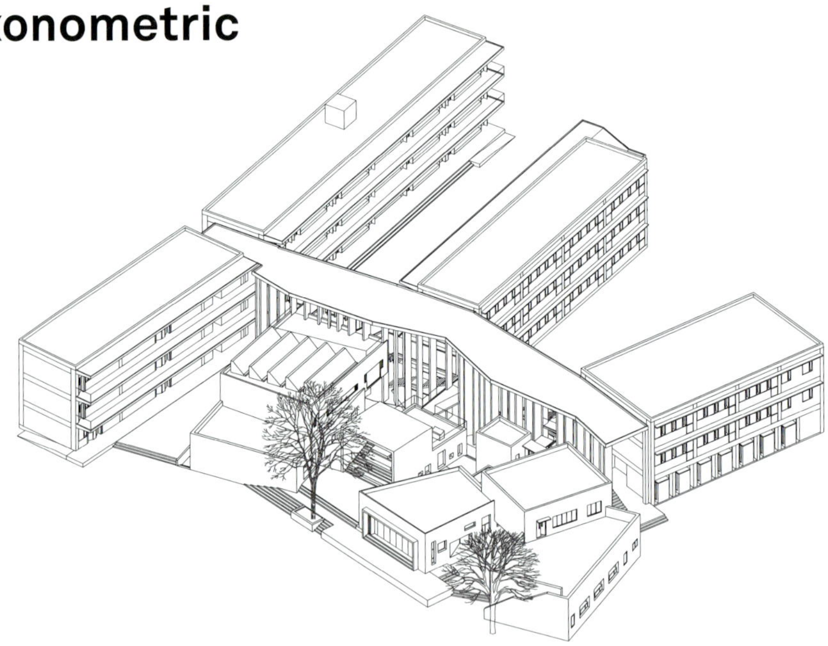

0

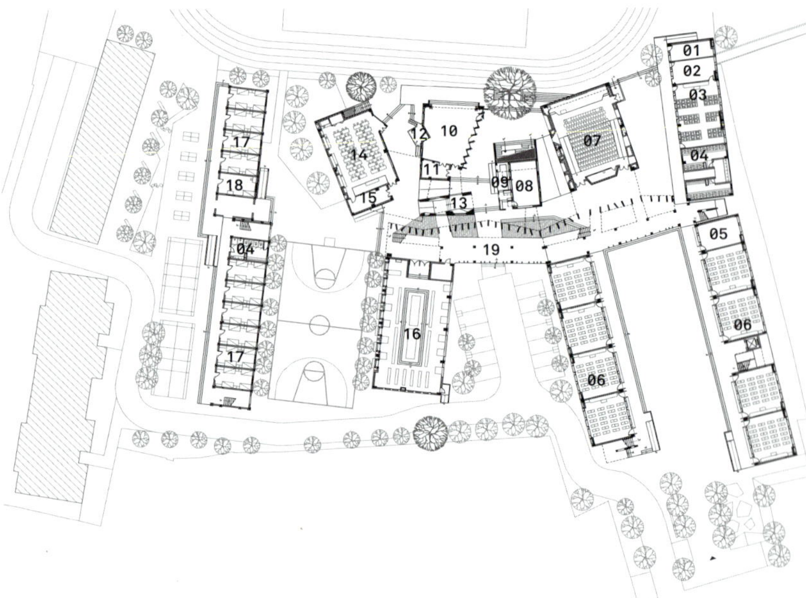

'Returning to a completed project helps you to understand how it's used in daily life'

↖ The school is conceived as a cluster of small buildings that form a micro city-like campus.

↗ The fragmentary composition of the school creates elements reminiscent of city life, such as streets, plazas, courtyards and steps.

→ Small corners and labyrinthine spaces provoke children's curiosity and imagination and encourage them to play.

↓ Sunshades, natural ventilation and other methods of heat reduction respond to Sichuan's hot and humid climate.

Section

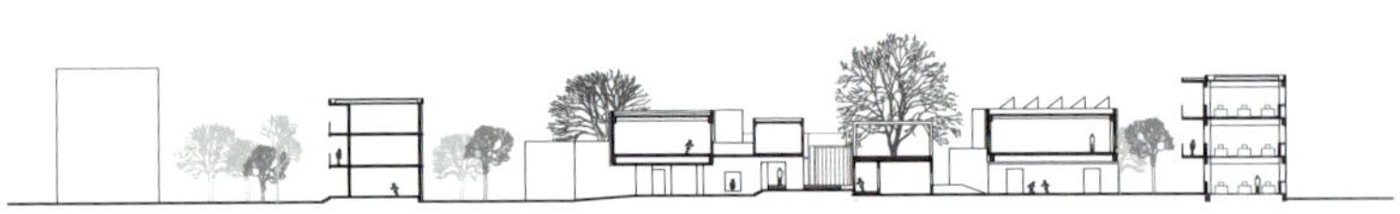

01 Sports room
02 Computer facilities
03 Computer room
04 Toilet
05 Teachers room
06 Classroom
07 Auditorium
08 Group-activity room
09 Play space
10 Music classroom
11 Musical-instruments room
12 Slide
13 Pavilion
14 Experimentation room
15 Preparation room
16 Reading room
17 Dormitory
18 Duty room
19 Corridor

Xiaoquan Elementary School

Xiaoquan | Sichuan | China | 2010

The Xiaoquan Elementary School was severely damaged during the catastrophic Sichuan earthquake in 2008 and subsequently demolished. To replace it, TAO erected a new school of the same name in the centre of Xiaoquan Old Town: capacity 900 pupils. A major goal was to maximize the use of local resources and craftsmanship. Local materials such as wood, brick and bamboo were used for windows, walls and ceilings. Recycled bricks from the earthquake were laid to make the pavement. Walls feature cast-in-situ concrete that has been left exposed. All construction was done by a local contractor.

Photos Yao Li

Text
Michael Webb

A luxurious inn is Todd Saunders' latest contribution to Fogo Island.

Photos
Iwan Baan

At Home in the Wilderness

↑ The double-height restaurant offers a spectacular view of the North Atlantic Ocean.

↗ Somewhat sheltered from the elements is the terrace on the south side of the building, a spot ideal for catching the rays.

Fogo Island Inn is the latest in a series of buildings designed by Saunders Architecture to reinvigorate the economy of a tiny speck of land off the northeast coast of Newfoundland. Like most site-specific architecture, it grew out of a partnership between an enlightened client and a responsive architect. Zita Cobb was born to a poor fishing family in Fogo but moved on to Ontario, where she got a business degree and went to work for fibre-optics company JDS Fitel. Cobb became one of its highest-paid executives and, when she left in 2002, used her wealth to establish the Shorefast Foundation with her brother, Anthony. She interviewed architects to work with her and found the ideal candidate in Todd Saunders, a compatriot who left Newfoundland to establish his practice in Bergen, Norway. Though they are separated by 5,000 km of ocean, the two regions are physically similar, but Bergen is prospering and Fogo has been floundering since the 1992 Canadian moratorium on cod fishing. The island is hard to reach, and only 2,700 people live in scattered villages around the jagged coastline.

'A wood platform was built around the footprint during construction to protect the fragile landscape'

For Saunders, it was a homecoming. He shared Cobb's deep attachment to the simplicity and history of a place he had left, like her, in search of a decently paid job. In Bergen he can enjoy the same outdoor life in the mountains and on the water, creating houses and a few other structures that respond to local conditions. Saunders 'operates at the margins of modern architecture, a geographical periphery that has provided the freedom to explore form, material, and program, set adrift from any definable movement'. The quote is from Jonathan Bell, coauthor of a new monograph, *Todd Saunders: Architecture in Northern Landscapes*, which emphasizes the lovingly crafted quality of this architect's work.

On Fogo, Cobb chose sites for four artists' studios, each a short walk from a village where guest artists would live and forge links with the community. Saunders designed all four as variations on the vernacular saltbox. 'We built the Long Studio first to see whether local builders could handle unfamiliar designs,' says Saunders (*Mark* 28, page 64). 'They quickly proved they could, and the other three were built simultaneously.' The abstract geometric forms of Twisted Tower, Bridge, and the trapezoidal Squish stand out as markers in the wilderness, enhancing its beauty. It's the same strategy that the Norwegian Roads Authority employed in commissioning new overlooks and visitors centres along remote scenic routes. To avoid the faux rustic kitsch that panders to sentimental tourists, selected architects were encouraged to propose bold interventions, as Saunders did in his dramatic Aurland Lookout: an arc of laminated wood that juts over a deep fjord.

Fogo Island Inn is located on an isolated granite headland. Saunders designed it from the inside out, wrestling with the floor plans to ensure a dramatic view for every guest, and accommodating the restaurant, lounge, bar, gym and conference centre as compactly as possible. His calculations generated an X-plan, with two short wings jutting from a four-storey bar. Entry-level spaces are limited to reduce the footprint and to allow the upper storeys to be supported on tilted steel poles.

The waterfront hotel is on Fogo Island, the largest of the offshore islands of Newfoundland and Labrador, Canada.

‘Fogo allows me to work hands-on with people I know’

The challenge was to construct a robust steel frame that would withstand Atlantic storms, while minimizing its mass. Saunders shares Glen Murcutt's conviction that buildings should sit lightly on the land, but sitting lightly can be only an illusion in a location as exposed as this one, where gales would topple any structure that was not firmly anchored. The slender poles suggest that the block is floating, and they evoke the wooden stilts that support fishermen's shacks, here as in Norwegian coastal villages. In both countries, this was an expedient born of necessity: the fishermen had no time or materials to build conventional foundations. Today, there's a choice, but the old way can still prove the best option. Foundations and framing for the inn had to be completed within a short building season on a remote site where everything has to be imported. ‘We sourced materials as close to home as possible and used Canadian spruce for cladding,’ recalls Saunders. ‘A wood platform was built around the footprint during construction to protect the fragile landscape, which can take centuries to renew itself at this latitude.’

The inn looks as though it has been around for a long time, and the lichened rocks are unscarred. In a village, it would loom over every building but the church, but in this vast horizontal expanse it feels modestly scaled. Most of the public spaces are accommodated in the two-storey east-west volume. They include a well-stocked library of books on the region, and a gallery curated by Fogo Island Arts where visitors can buy works created here by guest artists. The small cinema is partnered with the National Film Board of Canada, so there are plenty of diversions on stormy days. Remaining public rooms and the 29 guest rooms and suites are accommodated in the main block, mostly on the two upper levels. All have ocean views, and three are double-height. Secure behind the double glazing, guests have a front-row view of waves and passing whales, but they are encouraged to get out and explore the island. Laundry, storage and services are contained in an outbuilding with a roof that is tilted to maximize the exposure

↑ Most of the hotel rooms have freestanding beds with wide 'headboards' that double as cupboards.

↖ The library, right off the main lobby, features colourful bookshelves and furnishings.

of solar panels. It defines an entry court for the buggies that bring guests from the off-site car park.

In contrast with the studios, which are mostly intended as workspaces for individual use, the inn will have substantial impact, physically and economically, and it had to be carefully calibrated in size and content. There were few places for visitors to stay, and Cobb wanted a boutique hotel for sophisticated travellers who would immerse themselves in the culture and history of the island while supporting its economy. Rooms are pricey, but all the profits go to the islanders. If places are made too accessible, tourism can get out of hand and destroy their integrity, as has happened all around the Mediterranean and especially in the Aegean. Even Norway's pristine Lofoten Islands, located far above the Arctic Circle, are at risk from the development that a proposed international airport would spawn.

Happily, there's little chance of that happening on Fogo. It's hard to reach and likely to remain so. The Shorefast Foundation – named for the tether that links a cod trap to the shore – works closely with the islanders. 'Our motivation is the well-being of this place and the people who live here,' says Cobb. She is talking to Saunders about a workshop that will allow the six ageing wood-boat builders to pass on their skills to a younger generation. Few on the island know how to swim, for the waters are cold and treacherous, A heated outdoor swimming pool is a high priority. Two more artists' studios are in the pipeline. 'Fogo is special, and it allows me to work hands-on with people I know,' says Saunders. 'Here in Bergen it's the same: I stop by every morning at eight to chat to the carpenters who are building my new house.' The architect's practice is flourishing, and he's building as far afield as Morocco, Turkey and the western United States. Success has brought him wide recognition, but he is determined to keep his office small enough to permit his personal involvement in every project. ←

saunders.no

+1

01 Gym
02 Housekeeping-manager's office
03 Staff lunchroom
04 Locker room
05 Toilets
06 Open to below
07 Conference room
08 Manager
09 Storage
10 Lobby
11 A/V room
12 Cinema
13 Study
14 Public lift
15 Service lift
16 Guest room
17 Mechanical chase

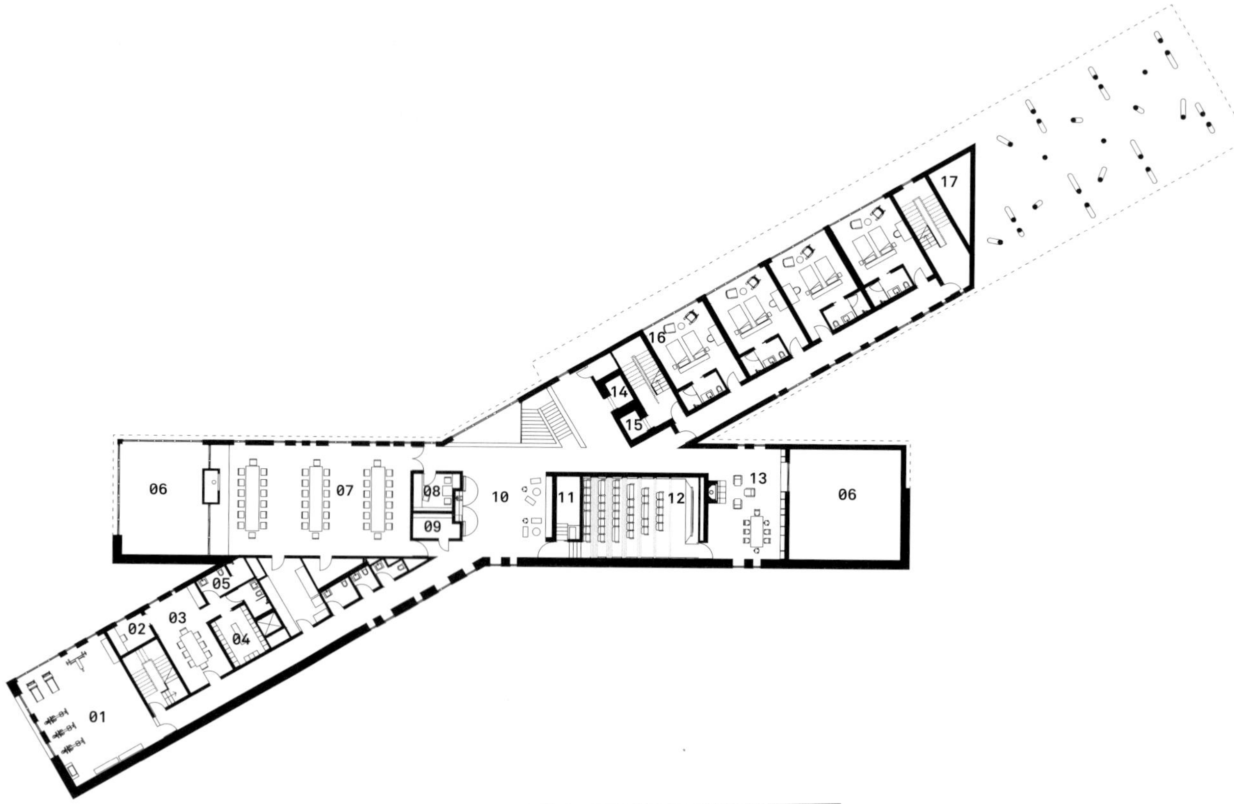

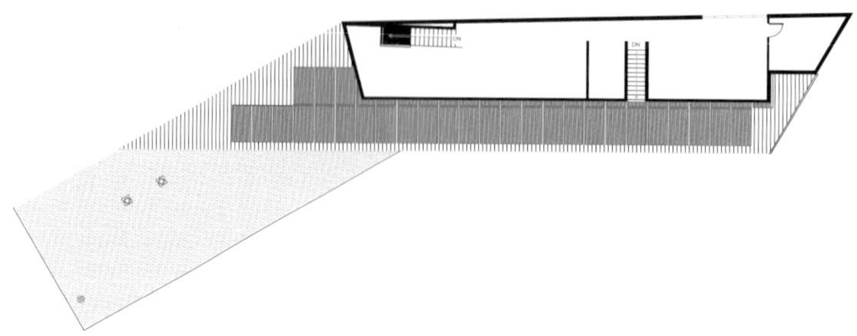

0

01 Restaurant
02 Lounge
03 Bar
04 Office
05 Coats
06 Toilets
07 Kitchen
08 Chef's office
09 Mechanical room
10 Main lobby
11 South entry
12 Library
13 Gallery
14 Lift lobby
15 Public lift
16 Service lift
17 Guest room
18 Mechanical chase
19 Boiler-tank room
20 Wood-boiler room
21 Wood-storage room
22 Generator and fuel-tank room
23 Transformer room
24 Chiller room
25 Restaurant storage
26 Water tank
27 Laundry and linen
28 Luggage storage
29 Dog-grooming room
30 Maintenance workshop
31 Recycling and refuse storage
32 Guest outerwear
33 Propane storage
34 Terrace

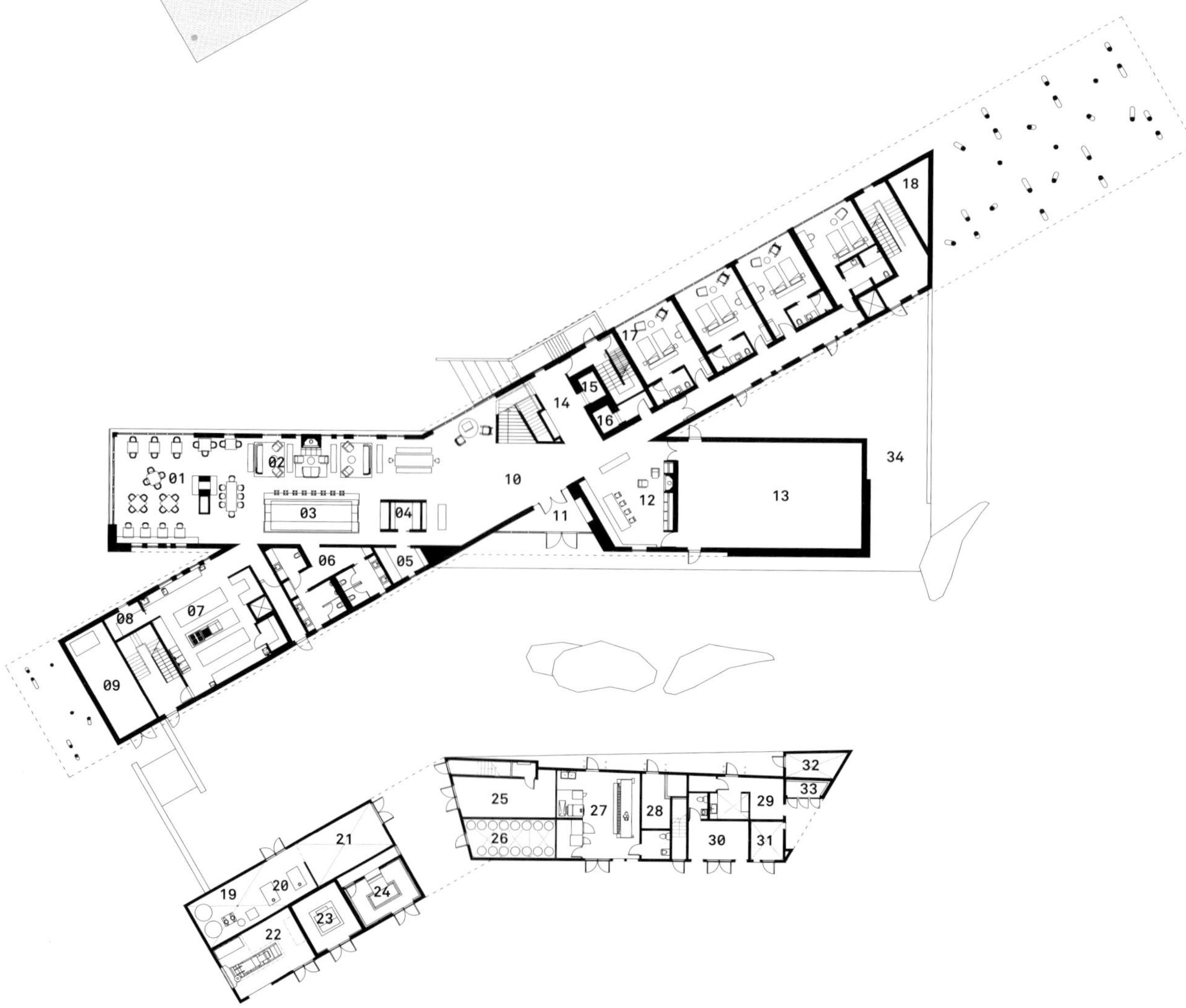

+3

01 Sauna
02 Chill-out area
03 Showers
04 Dry-off area
05 Dressing room
06 Toilets
07 Lobby
08 Covered outdoor area
09 Roof terrace
10 Lift lobby
11 Linen
12 Public lift
13 Service lift
14 Guest room
15 Mechanical room

'We sourced materials as close to home as possible'

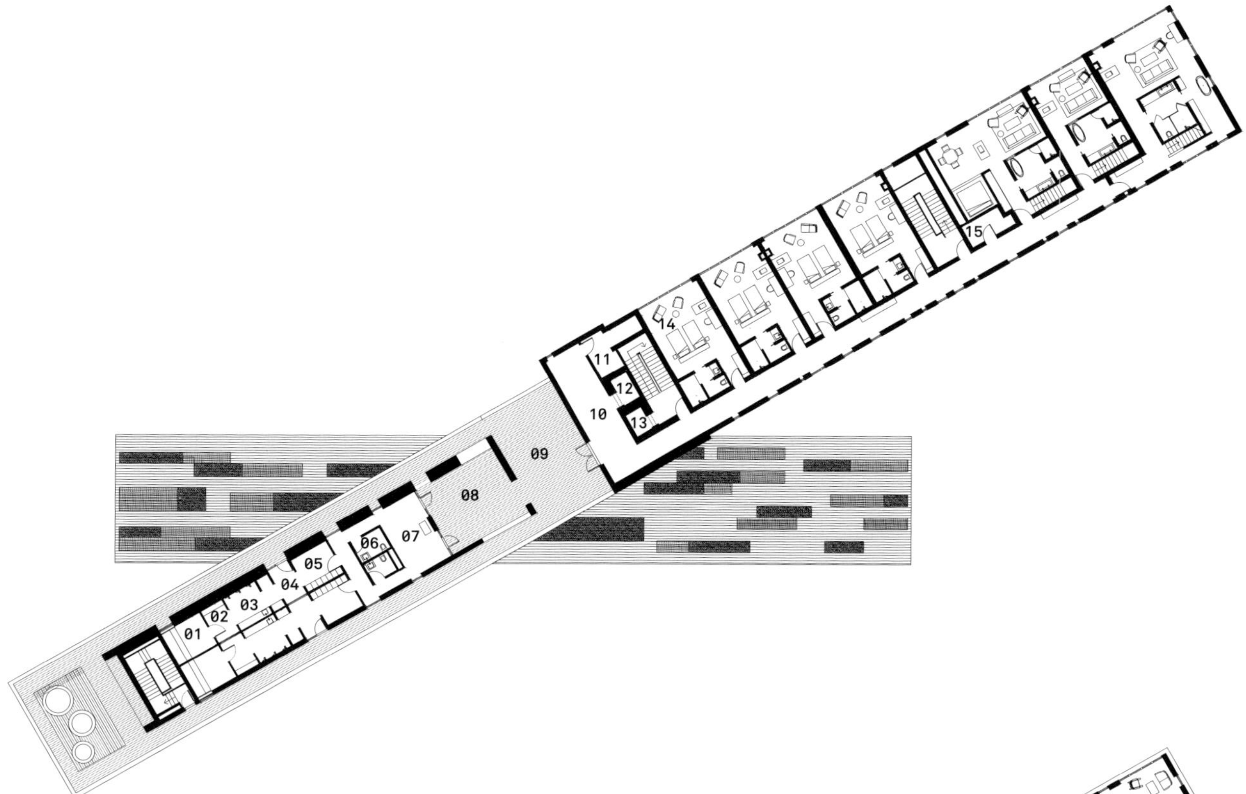

+2

01 Guest room
02 Linen
03 Public lift
04 Service lift
05 Mechanical room

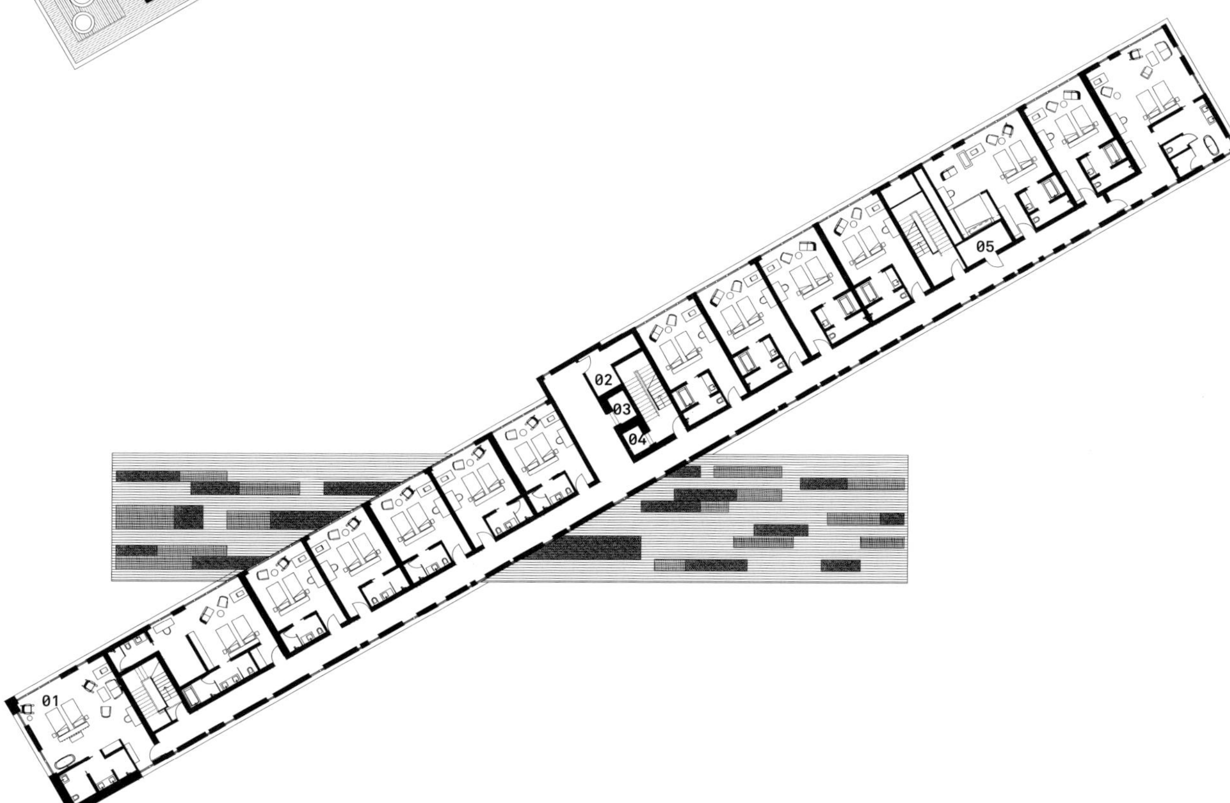

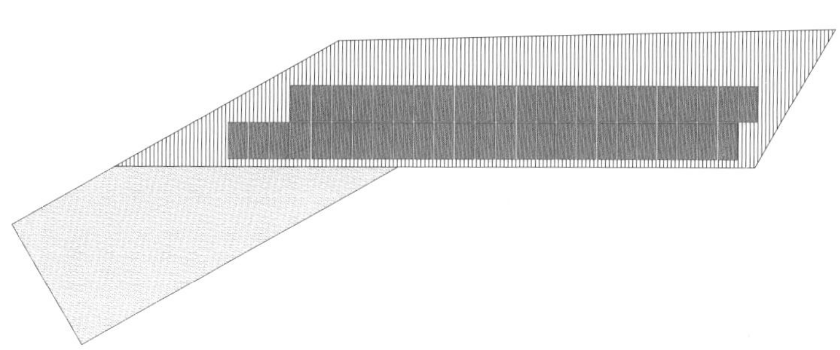

Text
Katya Tylevich

Photo
Alexei Tylevich

'Journalism still rewards your curiosity'

According to Christopher Hawthorne, a fresh breeze is fluttering the pages of architecture criticism, bringing a renewed focus to the political dimension of architecture.

B

Before coming to the *Los Angeles Times* in 2004, Christopher Hawthorne was the architecture critic for *Slate*, a frequent contributor to *The New York Times*, a contributing editor for *Metropolis*, and the coauthor of *The Green House: New Directions in Sustainable Architecture* (2005). His by-line, therefore, has ridden the waves of online traffic, magazine circulation, a newspaper of record and a hardcover – publications with different readers, different ambitions and different voices, though Hawthorne's stays consistently his, no matter the outlet.

As a critic, Hawthorne has a reputation for being well researched, measured and direct. Of course, 'direct' – what a snowflake – is a word that is its own unique euphemism for 'fair' or 'harsh', depending on who's throwing the snowball. When 'direct' is used to describe Hawthorne's approach, it's usually shorthand for saying he's clear in his opinions, honest about the way he's arrived at them and exact in his language. →

Christopher Hawthorne.

← **When we meet in Downtown Los Angeles at a café by the *LA Times* office, Hawthorne is quick to point out that strong opinions aren't necessarily rigid ones. The critics he respects most, like Ada Louise Huxtable, are those known to have revisited and challenged their beliefs. He talks at length about his distaste for unnecessary complexity, a kneejerk reaction he developed as a student in the age of postmodernism's rise and one that shapes his views of the do's and don'ts of criticism today.**

A few days before our meeting, I'd attended a talk Hawthorne gave at LACMA (Los Angeles County Museum of Art), in which he discussed American architecture's relationship with nature in the last half century. After Hawthorne had taken questions from the audience and bid his farewell, I heard the person behind me marvel: 'He's so easy to understand!' Thanks, stranger, for stressing how much of a novelty it still is for the general public to feel included in architectural discourse, and for foreshadowing the key points of my conversation with Hawthorne about why that fact is changing.

Why is it a high compliment to call an architecture critic 'comprehensible'? Isn't that part of the job description?

CHRISTOPHER HAWTHORNE: Architecture naturally cuts across many boundaries – it touches on aesthetics, urbanism, real estate, physics and economics. By definition, if you're writing about architecture you're writing for a number of different audiences. And yes, the job of a newspaper critic is to produce criticism that's legible and clear, especially when explaining obscure, difficult architectural concepts. But the pendulum swings back and forth between moments when the profession is trying to close ranks and think about how it talks just to itself, and moments when it wants to open the conversation to others. I came of age in a moment when it was all about closing ranks and figuring out who's in the room and qualifies as a true believer.

What moment was that?

When I was studying architectural history, first as an undergraduate at Yale in the early 1990s, and then as part of a fellowship programme at Columbia in 1998. I clearly remember being at absolutely packed symposia and panels. I'd wait two hours to get in, then leave incredibly frustrated. Even as someone who'd been studying architectural history and theory for quite some time, I felt the conversations were geared to foreclose any kind of clarity. Now, I think we're seeing a reaction against that – not just in criticism but in architecture itself. The architecture being produced when I was a student put a premium on formal distance and complexity, matching the rhetoric and theory of the moment.

And you're referring to ...?

Peter Eisenman, of course, certain postmodernists and other architects of the same generation – Thom Mayne, Eric Owen Moss, others in the LA School – who share a kind of distrust of clarity and whose work aimed to be tough and in certain ways unapproachable. There was, and still is, a sense among that generation that if something's clear, it's intellectually suspect and suggests a kind of naivety. The generational shift I see now is a response to that. The architects and landscape architects doing the work I find most interesting now – redesigning a waterfront to anticipate sea-level rise, say – are so engaged in grappling with real environmental, cultural and political complexity that they don't need to lay a complex formal language over the top, like an applique, the way Eisenman or Thom Mayne might. For them it would look silly – not just dated but entirely redundant and disconnected from the architectural and social issues at hand.

On the other hand, is the internet driving an oversimplification of architectural concepts? Critics and architects today have to reconcile with projects being understood as images without words. They also come face to face with the public's comments.

Well, for most of its 20th-century history, LA was kind of like the internet: its sense of openness and lack of central authority gave room for experimentation, which produced a lot of great architecture, as well as a lot of ugliness. Digital culture is the same, in many ways. It allows more things to come to the surface, which is both good and bad.

In face of that, as this generation's critics, we have to broaden our definition of what innovation means. It might not be a project that *looks* particularly innovative on a website or in a magazine. It's hard for us to learn that lesson, because we've been trained otherwise, but the projects I find disappointing are the ones that are a theatrical façade – a kind of billboard of experimentation that's not actually being pursued. We'll have to find ways to get off that treadmill, which is a conversation already in progress.

While you were navigating opaque theory as a student, which critics shined a light?

Most of all, Ada Louise Huxtable, with her combination of toughness and clarity. No one could accuse her of being naive about the political implications of how buildings get made in New York. There was real directness, even bluntness to the language she used. Early on, she was establishing her authority at a moment when the notion of authority was under attack, first in the broader culture in the '60s and then in architecture in the '70s and '80s. In her later works, though, she also reached a point where she could be very honest about the process of changing her mind, which is not something you see too often among critics. I find that refreshing. For all the problems that come with journalism now and all the anxiety about the future of journalism, it's still a place that rewards your curiosity and allows you to follow it.

As opposed to what other place?

Academia, where I find you get rewarded for carving out your own piece of turf and defending it against all comers. There's not really an incentive to figure out how the world has changed or how your view might have changed.

'Architects and critics are struggling with the fact that they were complicit in a lot of boom-time thinking'

For example, one book that's still hugely important and influential for me is *City of Quartz* [1990] by Mike Davis, but it came out 20 years ago and LA has changed drastically in that time. I would love to see what Davis makes of how the city's trying to grapple with its public realm again, in ways that actually cut against his thesis. Instead, I think – in a way typical for academics – he's applying that same thesis to other parts of the world, writing about Dubai or slums in India the same way he wrote about landscapes of exclusion in Los Angeles. I think academia rewards you for doing that sort of thing. As opposed to what Ada Louise was able to do later in her career, when she revisited her feelings about buildings and architects. I've been thinking a lot about what happened to her very certain critical voice when she encountered her doubts, when the world of architecture was going through such a change in the '70s. I think we're in another moment now, when the field is struggling to redefine itself.

Struggling with what?

In the aftermath of the economic collapse, architects and critics are struggling with the fact that they were complicit in a lot of boom-time thinking. For years, architects were working for a smaller part of society and getting more attention by doing so. In some ways, they became famous without becoming more influential and actually saw their political powers wane. It wasn't just the economic collapse that exposed that – it was the process of rebuilding the World Trade Center, as well as what happened after Hurricane Katrina. Those were the two Waterloo moments when we had to confront head-on the impotence of the profession and of criticism as it had evolved before 2008. I was writing about the WTC rebuilding process before I came to the *LA Times*, and that moment really exposed the limitations of a lot of critics, myself included.

What kinds of limitations?

We were exposed for our inability to cover that story with the breadth it deserved, which meant writing about real estate, politics, geopolitics, intensely local New York politics, land use, the idea of memorials – plus the idea of architecture, celebrity architecture and culture all wrapped together.

I think that for all the ways Herbert Muschamp [*The New York Times* architecture critic 1992-2004] could be brilliant, even he wasn't equipped to talk about the rebuilding process in a way that, in my opinion, it needed to be talked about. I don't know that he could have turned the process around single-handedly – that may be giving criticism too much credit – but he was in a position to attempt to shift the conversation and ask whether by insisting on rebuilding all 10 million square feet of the original towers we were about to repeat the mistakes made in the 1970s when the WTC buildings went up for the first time, stood empty, and had to be filled with state employees.

Hurricane Katrina brought a similar realization about how limited criticism and maybe architectural practice had gotten: how ill-equipped our conversation was to deal with a broader set of questions, which in New Orleans also includes those of history, preservation and regional ecology. Architectural criticism moved away from talking in those broad terms. Having realized that, I think there's been a significant effort by a group of today's critics to pull the focus back out a little bit and think about the various ways that architecture operates, particularly in a political sense.

Besides you, who are some of those critics?

I think Blair Kamin [*Chicago Tribune*] had been doing a broader approach in Chicago for a while. I think John King [*San Francisco Chronicle*] has done something similar. Paul Goldberger [*Vanity Fair*], especially in writing about New York, understands the complexities of the political environment. In my generation, Mark Lamster [*Dallas Morning News*] and Alexandra Lange. And the approach Michael Kimmelman's taken at *The New York Times* applies some of those lessons, as he's come into a completely new position – in his case, moving from art to architecture.

Are these limitations and realizations specific to the United States, or is this conversation happening globally?

It's absolutely global, and it's tied to moments of global economic and environmental crisis. There have been similar conversations in Japan after Fukushima and in Europe after the economic crisis. I'm more familiar with the conversation among young architects in Europe than among critics there, and I find there's been an attempt to redefine what an architectural practice means in the same way young critics here are trying to redefine the field in which criticism operates. You see it playing out in the last two [Venice] Architecture Biennales, particularly Sejima's in 2010, and in the way the curatorial approach at MoMA New York has changed, with exhibitions like '9+1 Ways of Being Political'. Even bringing in the word 'political' used to be taboo in architecture – an objection that just seems quainter and quainter, the further we get.

You still come across the 'taboo'?

I've been in reviews with people who get angry and emotional if anyone tries to raise a political line of questions about a student's project. They see architecture school as a place where the discussion ought to be just about architecture itself – as a way to give the students a protected place to operate, I suppose. The irony, of course, is that many of those same people think of themselves as inherently political, even radical – coming out of 1968, shaped by the political events of that year and the years that followed. Having come out of real engagement and activism, they seem stuck in a cul-de-sac, increasingly detached from any relevant kind of politics. But maybe 20 years from now young critics will say the same thing about my generation. Some of that is probably inevitable. In the end, it comes to every generation to point out the limitations and blind spots of the one that came before. ←

Christopher Hawthorne Comments on Books about Los Angeles

Carey McWilliams, *Southern California: An Island on the Land.* Published in 1946 and still the best book ever written about the culture, history and built environment of Los Angeles.

Piecing Together Los Angeles: An Esther McCoy Reader (2012). Collected essays and reviews by LA's first and finest architecture critic, who died in 1989.

Reyner Banham, *Los Angeles: The Architecture of Four Ecologies.* Published in 1971, the first book by an outsider – in this case the British architecture historian and critic – to understand, dissect and celebrate Los Angeles on its own terms. LA boosterism at its most gregariously intelligent.

D.J. Waldie, *Holy Land: A Suburban Memoir* (1996). A brilliantly structured meditation on growing up in Lakewood, the first planned community in Southern California. A family memoir that is also a sharp analysis of LA's affection for the single-family house.

Douglas R. Suisman, *Los Angeles Boulevard: Eight X-Rays of the Body Public* (1989). Suisman's underappreciated study of LA's major streets will soon be published in a new edition to mark its 25th anniversary. I was very pleased to be asked to write the introduction for the new version, as the book was a significant influence on my own recent *LA Times* essays on the boulevards.

Charles Moore (with Peter Becker and Regula Campbell), *The City Observed: Los Angeles* (1998). A winningly idiosyncratic architecture guidebook. Moore's writing holds up far better than his buildings.

Anna Deavere Smith, *Twilight: Los Angeles, 1992* (1994). A play that captures the riot-torn landscape of 1990s Los Angeles as well as any piece of architectural or cultural history.

William Alexander McClung, *Landscapes of Desire: Anglo Mythologies of Los Angeles* (2000). A study, in effortless prose, of how white America took control of Los Angeles in the 1850s, justified that control in politics and culture for more than a century, and then lost it sometime in the 1980s.

Richard Meltzer's Guide to the Ugliest Buildings of Los Angeles (1980). Meltzer, a pioneering rock critic, moonlighted in the 1970s as an architecture critic for the *LA Reader*, writing memorably about the city's seemingly bottomless collection of architectural offenders.

Tools

Wienerberger decides award winners

Every other year, the international Wienerberger Brick Award, initiated in 2004, goes to outstanding examples of modern and innovative brick architecture. This year again, international architecture critics and journalists were invited to submit extraordinary brick buildings for the 2014 Wienerberger Brick Award. Relevant criteria included an innovative architectural design and excellent craftsmanship in the use of bricks, as well as functionality, sustainability and energy efficiency.

On 1 June 2013, an international jury of experts, invited by Wienerberger, met in Vienna for the final selection of the award-winning projects. As in previous years, the jury included architects of international renown – foremost among them Pritzker Prize winner Wang Shu (China), Vera Yanovshtchinsky (the Netherlands), Ewa Kuryłowicz (Poland) and Pavol Paňák (Slovakia). 'I am very happy that Wienerberger succeeded in winning international star architects like Wang Shu as jury members for its Brick Award. We regard the Wienerberger Brick Award not only as a distinction for architects working with bricks, a natural building material, in an exemplary fashion, but also as a means of promoting an international exchange of ideas on the brick architecture of the future. Our jury of renowned architects from Europe and Asia is ideally placed to communicate our message,' says Johann Windisch, CEO of Bricks & Tiles Europe, Wienerberger AG.

Five categories qualify for the Brick Award. One of the five award-winning projects is then selected for the grand prize. Out of a total of 300 entries, 50 projects from 26 countries were nominated for the 2014 Brick Award. The jury selected the winners of prizes in each of the five categories and the winner of the grand prize. In particular, the jury focused on projects involving a substantial research and innovation effort, as well as on projects stemming from pioneering technologies or contributing to an improvement of the quality of life.

'Wienerberger had absolutely no say in the selection of projects; the only thing that counts is the assessment by the jury of experts,' says Windisch, underlining the objectivity of the procedure. Heimo Scheuch, CEO of Wienerberger AG, is convinced that the award conveys an important message: 'As in previous years, the award-winning projects illustrate the great variety of applications for clay as a natural building material in architecture. Brick buildings are healthy, economical and energy-efficient – features that are bound to gain in importance for future-oriented architecture.'

The Brick Award ceremony will take place on 8 May 2014 in Vienna. Buildings pictured are a random selection from the list of nominations.

wienerberger.com

↖ **Paasitorni Hotel, Paasitorni, Finland, by K2S Architects (Kimmo Lintula, Mikko Summanen and Niko Sirola).**
Photo Marko Huttunen

↗ **Ravensburg Art Museum, Ravensburg, Germany, by Lederer Ragnarsdóttir Oei.**
Photo Roland Halbe

← **The jury. From left to right: Ewa Kuryłowicz, Wang Shu, Pavol Paňák and Vera Yanovshtchinsky.**
Photo Christian Dusek

→ **Urban Collage, Champigny-sur-Marne, Paris, France, by Maison Edouard François.**
Photo Paul Raftery

↓ **Tongjiang Primary School, Xiaosong, Jiangxi, China, by Rural Urban Framework (John Lin and Joshua Bolchover)**
Photo RUF

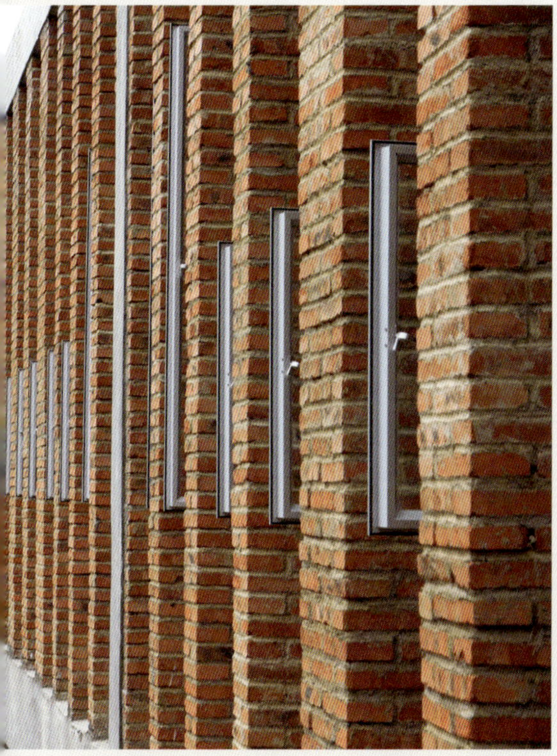

Alucobond mirrors the past

A

At the edge of the German town of Schöningen, known for its open-cast lignite mine, is the site of a world-famous Stone-Age discovery: the remarkable Schöningen Spears, which are the oldest completely preserved hunting weapons ever found. Now located at the same spot is the new Paläon complex, an emblematic research and experience centre that is visible from a considerable distance away. Designed by Holzer Kobler Architekturen, the building rises above the natural topography like layered earth, thus communicating the archaeological importance of the location. The building's futuristic shape appears to evolve from the horizontal plane, referencing the landscape while flaunting the lines that define its volume, ground plan and section. Its offset forms create subtly different internal and external spaces.

Meticulously designed, the Paläon is clad in reflective Alucobond®, which makes the building a mirror for the landscape. Large, deeply incised ribbon fenestration suggests shadows across the building and underscores the expressive dynamism of the architecture, while offering to those inside views of the nearby woods and wild horses and, farther off, the mine and the site of the exciting find. The extended axes of the building resemble linear tracks moving into the landscape, where they link up, synapse-like, with the network of paths in the surrounding park.

alucobond.com

↙ **The building is clad in Alucobond®Plus Reflect.**

→ **Archaeological finds from the area around Schöningen are on display inside the building.**

↓ **Landscape architects PBR and Topotek1 designed the outdoor spaces.**
Photos Alucobond | Jan Bitter

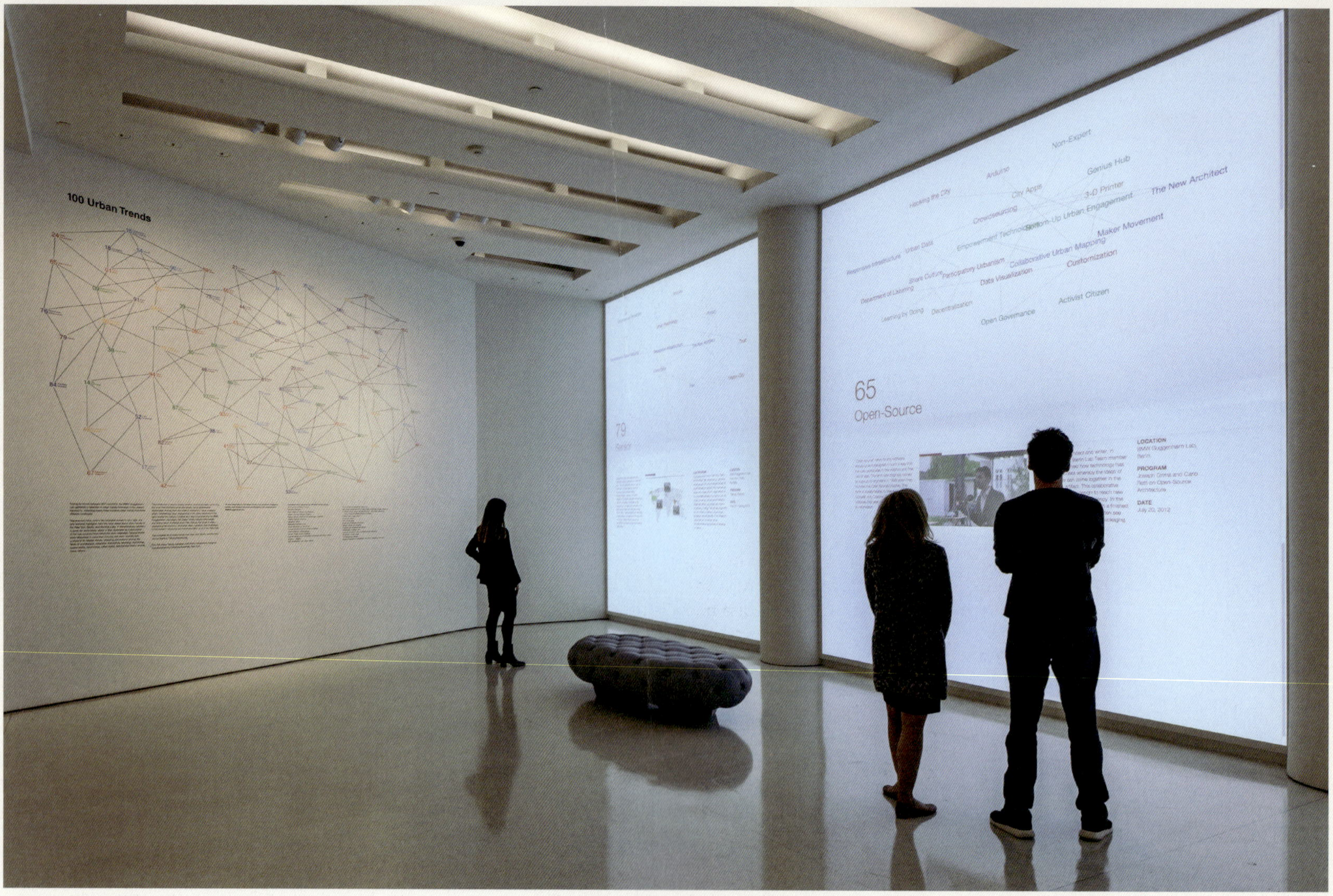

Text
David Keuning

The city according to **BMW** and **Guggenheim**

The BMW Guggenheim Lab has had a bumpy history. In the autumn of 2011, when the German carmaker and the American museum opened the original lab in New York City – inside a mobile pavilion designed by Atelier Bow-Wow – their ambitions were sky-high (*Mark* 40, pages 130-131). After the stint in New York, the pavilion looked forward to a tour of the world, with stops in Berlin, Mumbai and six other major cities. Two more architecture firms were to design pavilions for future sites. The lab would 'raise awareness of important issues, generate specific ideas for particular cities, and explore ideas and solutions related to sustainable design, yielding lasting benefits for cities around the world'.

What actually happened was something altogether different. The location selected for the pavilion in Berlin, in the neighbourhood of Kreuzberg, aroused so much protest – in the form of media polemics and demonstrations – that BMW and the Guggenheim eventually opted for a site in Prenzlauerberg, a more peaceful part of town. A statement issued by the Guggenheim Foundation included this explanation: 'While we welcome vigorous debate, we cannot risk the possibility of violence.' Dissidents in Berlin objected to the project because they didn't want a bunch of Americans and a Munich-based multinational telling them how to inhabit and use their city.

After appearances in New York City, Berlin and Mumbai, the remainder of the tour was cancelled. The Guggenheim Museum in New York is currently hosting 'Participatory City: 100 Urban Trends from the BMW Guggenheim Lab', the final exhibition in the series.

← **A view of the exhibition space at the Guggenheim Museum in New York City, where 100 of the more significant trends from the BMW Guggenheim Lab are highlighted in large wall projections.**
Photo Solomon R. Guggenheim Foundation

→ **The BMW Guggenheim Lab in New York City in 2011.**
Photo David Heald | Solomon R. Guggenheim Foundation

↓ **BMW Guggenheim Lab's 'Making Things Move' programme took place in Berlin on 16 June 2012.**
Photo Luke Abiol | Solomon R. Guggenheim Foundation

↓ **BMW Guggenheim Lab's 'Pop-Up Garden' programme took place in Mumbai on 21 December 2012.**
Photo UnCommonSense | Solomon R. Guggenheim Foundation

It's unclear whether the incident in Berlin is the reason for the project's premature termination. Speaking at the opening of the latest exhibition, Thomas Girst, who is the head of cultural engagement at BMW, skirted the issue by saying that 'it was an open project, despite the announcement'. BMW made the decision to stop 'for strategic reasons that always happen inside a big company'. The most obvious motive for discontinuing the project is a desire to minimize damage to BMW's reputation.

You could also call the lab a highly successful initiative precisely *because* of all the controversy it's caused, despite the fact that this type of polemic was not what the organizers had in mind. The exhibition is a reflection of the 300 topics discussed during activities that took place in the labs – subjects with titles such as Megacity, Urban Ugliness, Aging Population, Sustainability, 3-D Printing and Citizen Empowerment. Curator Maria Nicanor chose 100 of the more significant 'trends' and highlighted their importance in a series of three large wall projections. Other screens and panels shed light on special details or provide even more depth into the various themes through interviews and videos.

The exhibition is engaging, but it also reveals the limitations of the conventional museum setting. It is, after all, not art that is on display here. 'The difficulty of the exhibition was to capture something that is very performative,' says Nicanor. 'I think we will never do the events justice by bringing them back within the museum walls. But for this project it is crucial that we say: these were the ideas that came out of it.' Despite the outcry in Germany, she's convinced of the project's overall success. 'There is such a hunger for cities and the people in them. Art can sometimes be intimidating, but we all live in cities; we all experience cities in our everyday lives. So people jump in. That was what made this experience interesting. It wasn't about an expert saying: this is how you're going to live your life in your city, and these are the five solutions you need to go by. It was completely the other way around. It was based on non-expert interaction.'

Seen from that perspective, the whole initiative takes on an open-ended character, and the same ambiguous air pervades the exhibition and lingers in your mind as you leave the museum. Ultimately, we all want a sustainable city, just as we all know that parts of Europe are being forced to cope with an ageing population. The labs did manage to produce a few concrete results in the cities where they appeared. The most successful outcome was in Mumbai. 'It turned out that there was one traffic node in the city that was incredibly dangerous for people to cross,' says Nicanor. 'The lab team organized a design competition to solve this infrastructural problem. We invited local transportation officials to help evaluate the entries and to commit to implementing the winning design, which they did. We also created a prototype of a bench that collects rainwater, designed by Dutch architect Neville Mars.' Benches developed from this prototype are being used in the city parks of Mumbai.

If the organizers' aim was to discover and realize improvements of this kind, why not invest money directly into urban development and skip the travelling labs? The project and the accompanying exhibition are bursting with good intentions, but the passion that the Guggenheim and BMW poured into this project also expresses a sense of naivety. Themes related to urban infrastructure, like Electric Cars, immediately point a suspicious finger at BMW and its impact on the project. (Thomas Girst firmly denies, however, that BMW had any influence on the content of the labs and their various programmes.) Then, too, it can be very difficult to present such abstract themes and activities in a museum setting. The task is comparable to that of recording a concert or a dance performance. It's always better when you're there in person.

guggenheim.org

'Participatory City: 100 Urban Trends from the BMW Guggenheim Lab' is on view at the Guggenheim Museum in New York City until 5 January 2014.

Mark Magazine 2012

Package Deal

A year's worth of issues, filled with up-to-the-minute inspiration from architects around the world. 6 issues €69 (Normal price €119.70)

Goods

Interior Products from Sketch to Use

***Goods* is a 500-page tome of product design that analyses the design process of 59 iconic objects. Follow a product's journey from conception to completion, and see the interiors that they form an essential part of.** Price €59

Think Dutch

Conceptual architecture and design in the Netherlands

***Think Dutch* presents and describes over 450 architectural projects and product designs devised by the most creative contemporary minds. They afford impressive proof of cutting-edge thinking, and show that future-oriented visions are arising out of crisis in the Netherlands.** Price €119

Exit

Mark 48
February | March 2014

Langarita-Navarro

Langarita-Navarro Arquitectos is a Spanish firm founded in 2005 by María Langarita and Victor Navarro, who talk to *Mark* about three of their striking new buildings, among which MediaLab Prado in Madrid. MediaLab is a cultural complex housed in the so-called 'Belgian Sawmill', one of the first architectural projects in Madrid to employ reinforced concrete. María Langarita: 'The existing building is made of heavy concrete, and the weight of the structure is conducted vertically to the foundations. Our new addition is transparent, made of plywood and textile, and suspended. We tried to use materials that didn't exist when the old building was erected at the beginning of the 20th century.'

Also

A look at Chinese construction companies building new towns in Kenya
An interview with location scout Toni Maier

And

New architecture in Denmark